Praise for *Co*

Socrates faced death, saying
living." Molly Lackey helps us live life (as well as face death) by examining ourselves in light of who Christ is and what He has done for us. Plumbing the central truths of Scripture in eminently accessible fashion, she leads her readers to know themselves as God knows them in Christ. She faithfully teaches that life examined in light of Christ is worth living now and for eternity.

—**Rev. Dr. Kevin Golden**, associate professor of exegetical theology, Concordia Seminary, St. Louis

Catechesis in the Church can sometimes be reduced to making sure a person can define the "big words" we use on Sundays, but in our world of chaos and confusion, Molly very simply puts forward the truth of your identity as being found in Jesus and in Him alone. Who is Jesus and why does His work matter, you ask? *Confessing Jesus* does exactly that: it candidly confesses Jesus—His life, death, and resurrection—and grounds your life and hope in Him. With discussion questions at the end of each chapter, *Confessing Jesus* is helpful for individual study or groups.

—**Rev. John Bussman**, senior pastor, St. Paul's Lutheran Church and School, Cullman, AL

Whether you've been Lutheran for one year, eighty years, or anywhere in between, Molly presents our core theology of "Jesus for you" in an engaging, relatable, and honest way. She retells our story of salvation with toe-holds for every reader, with a beautifully clear exposition of Law and Gospel. In our rapidly changing culture and sometimes overwhelmingly confusing world, Molly's words about who we are in Christ and His creation bring a delightful and introspective pause in order to refocus on what Christ has done for us, why that's a big deal, and how we can rest in Him.

—**Sarah Gulseth**, digital media specialist, KFUO Radio

A lot of energy is being spent in our current culture to know one's identity. Things become even more problematic when individuals turn inward for answers. This is why Mrs. Lackey's book, *Confessing Jesus*, is so incredibly pertinent, timely, and helpful. With a refreshing writing style, combined with a deep knowledge of Scripture, culture, and history, Mrs. Lackey turns a searching culture outward to the who, what, where, when, and why of Jesus. But how does confessing Jesus address identity? Mrs. Lackey wonderfully answers this in the pages of *Confessing Jesus*, saying, "To know ourselves, we must first know Christ." Indeed, Mrs. Lackey's gem of a book gets all of us to the core of our identity—hearing and knowing how Jesus defines us.

—**Rev. Dr. Matthew Richard**, pastor of St. Paul's Lutheran Church of Minot, ND, and author of *Will the Real Jesus Please Stand Up? 12 False Christs* and *Minute Messages: Gospel-Filled Devotions for Every Occasion*.

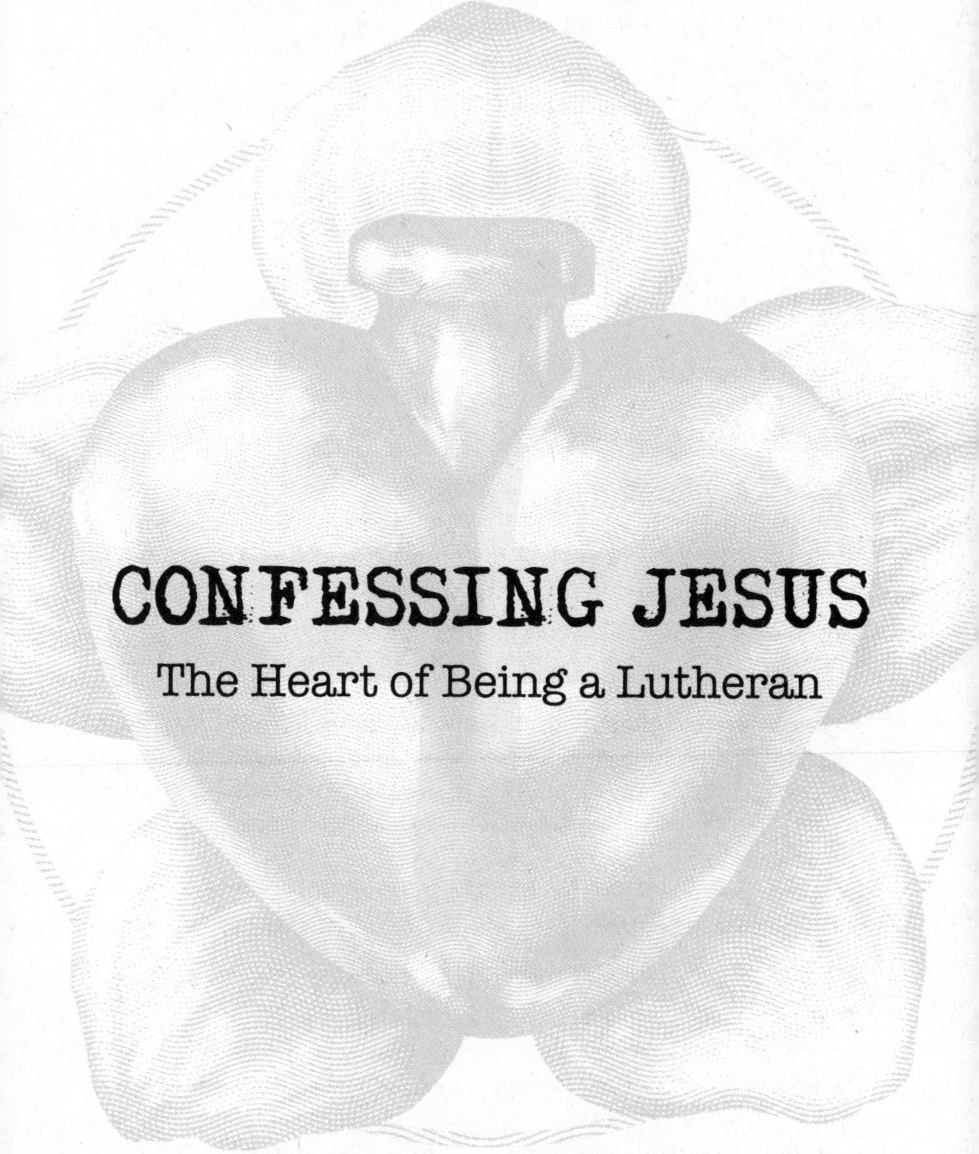

CONFESSING JESUS

The Heart of Being a Lutheran

MOLLY LACKEY

Published by Concordia Publishing House
3558 S. Jefferson Avenue, St. Louis, MO 63118-3968
1-800-325-3040 • cph.org

Manufactured in the United States of America

1 2 3 4 5 6 7 8 9 10 31 30 29 28 27 26 25 24 23 22

ACKNOWLEDGMENTS

First and foremost, this book would not have been possible without my wonderful husband, Jonathan. Thank you for putting up with the endless "Can I bounce an idea off you?" conversations, for encouraging me when I was in the trenches, and for being the spiritual head and anchor of our little family. Thank you for your prayers and your words of comfort, especially during the difficult task of writing a first book. I love you and am so grateful for you.

No author is an island, and no book gets published without a host of people on the publishing side of things. My good friends at Concordia Publishing House have been utterly indispensable in the creation of this book. From my first brainstorming sessions to the final proofread, you have all been a Godsend. Thank you especially to Laura Lane, Wayne Palmer, Holli Rolfes, Anna Johnson, Denise Prange, and Jess Paterik.

Finally, I would like to give thanks to God for the life and work of Paul McCain, publisher and executive editor at CPH. I got to know Paul during my internship at CPH in the summer of 2019, and I treasure in my heart all those trips to his office to talk about Reformation history, theology, life as a Southern Lutheran, books I need to read, forgotten corners of Luther's *Table Talks*, and any and everything else. We continued a lively email correspondence afterward, and he was deeply encouraging and helpful in the early stages of this book's pitching and planning. After Paul's unexpected death in November 2020, I have lost count of how many times I have wanted to email him some Luther tidbit I found online or ask his advice on writing and on life. But I know that Paul's and my Redeemer lives, and I take great comfort in knowing that he rests in the arms of our Lord, who will raise him and all the faithful on the Last Day. I'm looking forward to it.

SOLI DEO GLORIA.

Table of Contents

INTRODUCTION

Do you know who you are?

That probably sounds like a weird question. Well, duh, I'm me! Sure. We all carry around a mental sack of facts that we pull out when we meet new people: name, hometown, marital status, vocation, occupation, kids, pets, hobbies, whatever. But that's not really who we *are,* is it? You're a lot more than where you live and what you do on weekdays. Unfortunately, our post-modern culture hasn't helped matters by preaching that you're defined by what you want; now, it seems like we're all defined by who we want in the White House, by who we want as a sexual partner, or by what we want—wealth, beauty, status, acceptance. With so many things by which to define ourselves, we seem to know who we actually are less and less and less.

Do you know who you are? A lot of people nowadays don't. Young and old alike are struggling with the constant shifting of culture, society, and even our own personalities. We can't define ourselves from within ourselves because the very nature of our lives means that we are always changing—growing up, growing old, changing where we live, changing where we work, changing our minds. Everything is always changing inside of us, so we need to look outside of ourselves to something that doesn't change in order to define ourselves. But where do we go? What do we need?

> ***Lord, to whom shall we go? You have the words of eternal life. Alleluia!***
> (*LSB*, p. 156, from John 6:68)

We turn to Jesus to find out who we are. Maybe that seems a little weird. We sometimes have a hard time connecting what we do in worship on Sundays—let alone complicated beliefs about who God is and the nature of salvation—with our "normal" lives and our "real life" selves. Sometimes pastors will talk about "Sunday morning disconnect," where people act one way at church and a completely different way the rest of the week. While this is a very real problem—we should strive to honor God and love our neighbor every day of the week, not just for an hour on Sunday morning—sometimes the problem is less open and obvious than immoral or unhelpful behaviors. Sometimes the problem is that we've become a patchwork of little identities, all warring for our full attention, our full devotion, our full selves. Maybe our external behaviors seem consistent and our friends and family think that we have it all together, but inside we're a jumbled mess. Maybe we do all the "right" things, but we don't know who we really are.

Jesus Christ defines who we really are. This is a core truth of our Christian faith.

Our status before the almighty God in eternity is defined by Jesus, and our own awareness of

ourselves is defined by how we think about Jesus. In order to know ourselves, we must first know Christ.

But like so many things in our postmodern world, it can feel like we have to figure out how to know Christ all on our own. That's a daunting task, to be sure. Maybe we have some success—or maybe (and usually) not—but it always feels like Jesus is a little *blurry*, far off, unreal, not well defined. We know some bits and pieces about Jesus, some cliché slogans or abstract terms, or maybe we just have some vague feelings, but they don't really all fit together. Jesus still feels far off and flat, like a character in an old, half-forgotten fable, or a distant object seen without much-needed glasses. As a result, we feel the same way about ourselves. We know a lot about ourselves—our interests, hobbies, skills, background, family tree—but somehow, we feel like we're missing something. We don't know Jesus, and so we don't know ourselves.

Thankfully, we don't have to figure out who Jesus is and why He matters alone. The title of this book, *Confessing Jesus*, attests to this. The word *confess* comes from the Latin verb *confiteor*, which means "to say together" or "to say completely." You see, if we try to talk about Jesus on our own, we always end up with an incomplete picture, a jigsaw puzzle with missing pieces. We put distance between ourselves and Christ and feel like strangers in our own souls because we can't possibly figure out the answers on our own. But when we speak about Jesus *together*, examining what the Church together has drawn from the Bible and taught about Jesus for the past two thousand or so years, we can also speak about Jesus *completely*, seeing a complete picture of Jesus—or, at least, as complete a picture as we can arrive at as frail, imperfect humans.

This desire to speak together about Jesus was also the driving motivation for Martin Luther behind the Protestant Reformation. Luther believed that inaccurate, nonscriptural teachings and practices had accumulated within the church of his day. It was his desire to go back to the basics, back to who Jesus is and what He has done for us, in hopes of getting a clearer picture of Jesus—and of himself.

Like a lot of people today, Luther was plagued by feelings of immense guilt, feelings that he couldn't seem to assuage no matter how much he tried to prove to himself and to others that he was a good person. But from the depths of his anxiety, fear, and guilt, he plunged back into the Scriptures, where he found Christ—and found out what Christ actually thought about him.

It was this clear, consoling image of Christ that drew me to the Lutheran faith. Like Luther, I had felt immense guilt—guilt that was unrelenting even in the face of my attempts to show my own goodness—and a sense that I didn't really know Jesus or myself. This book mirrors my own path from a confused understanding of Jesus to a bold confession of Christ, passed down to me by faithful pastors and teachers who opened the Word of God to me.

Maybe you've felt this way too. Sometimes, the bustle and changes of life can overtake or distract us, and pretty soon our image of Jesus becomes clouded, out of focus. Or maybe you've always had questions about your faith and your identity, but you haven't known quite how to ask them or where to start.

My hope with this book is to show you the real, comforting presence of Jesus, the heart of what it means to be Christian, especially as a Lutheran. It is a book by a layperson, for other laypeople, which I hope will spark a deeper understanding of and appreciation for who Jesus is. As such, it is not exhaustive. It might lead you to ask more questions, too, questions that I hope you will take to your pastor. Together, we'll dive deeply into five big questions that lie at the heart of Lutheran identity, drawing inspiration from the "Five *W*s" (Who? What? Where? When? Why?), those five most basic questions that we learn in elementary school to ask in order to fully know and understand something or someone. We'll ask these five questions:

Who is Jesus?

What did Jesus do?

Where is Jesus now?

When is Jesus coming back?

Why did Jesus do all this?

We'll consider each of these questions deeply, drawing from Scripture and our own Lutheran Confessions, which in turn were drawn from the faithful wisdom of countless Church Fathers and theologians from the preceding 1,500 years. As we meditate on Christ together, we'll come to see Jesus as He really is: present with you, even now, to comfort, rescue, and redeem you, now and for eternity. In the process, we'll also finally understand ourselves by seeing ourselves not in fragmented isolation and the ever-changing, always-refracting lens of the world, the devil, and our fallible, feeble selves, but rather through Christ, who has reconciled us to God and to our fellow brothers and sisters in Him.

But before we can know ourselves, we must first know Jesus. Like the Greek believers who approached Philip, we likewise say, "We wish to see Jesus" (John 12:21).

CHAPTER ONE

WHO IS JESUS?

Who is Jesus? This question is probably the most important question you've never asked. Maybe you already have, but for most people, Christian or not, they already have a lot of preconceived ideas about Jesus that keep them from asking this all-important question: "Who is Jesus?"

We're going to start from scratch in this chapter. We're going to answer this question by telling the story of Jesus in three different ways: Jesus as God, as man, and as God-man.

Of course, there aren't three different Jesuses. There is only one person of Jesus, both God and man, distinct from the Father and the Holy Spirit but united with them in the Trinity. Jesus does, however, have two "natures," by which we mean a certain set of characteristics that defines a category.

For example, cats have a nature. They have a set of experiences, abilities, and physical characteristics that make them all cats. Under normal conditions, your typical cat is supposed to skitter about with whiskers and a tail, have a more-or-less curious disposition, enjoy eating fish (or kitty food, as the case may be), and be good at hunting and catching things, whether that's mice or toys.

What sets Jesus apart as the most important and unique individual in all of history is that He has *two* natures: He has a human nature and a divine nature. This means that Jesus has the experiences, abilities, and other characteristics of a human, while also exhibiting the characteristics of God. He was born in time, and yet He was present at the birth of the universe; He grew in knowledge and stature, and yet He is all knowing, all present, and all powerful; He could (and would!) be harmed, injured, and killed, and yet He brought healing and life. He is both God and man, 100 percent each, simultaneously.

What this means is that Jesus is one *person*. When we say "person" here, we're not talking about a human individual. Rather, it's a way of referring to a unified essence or entity. We confess that "Jesus Christ is the same yesterday and today and forever" (Hebrews 13:8), but we also confess that Jesus took on a human body at a specific point in history, when He "was incarnate by the Holy Spirit of the virgin Mary" (Nicene Creed). Jesus existed before He became man, and His essence, or person, has remained the same throughout all time.

It is very important that we don't mix up Jesus' human nature and His divine nature because it is necessary that He be both God and man, not a fifty-fifty mixture. But it is also important that we don't act like there are two Jesuses, a human Jesus who died on the cross and a divine Jesus up in heaven. That's also wrong. That's why we'll be telling the story of Jesus three times: once to talk about His divine nature, once to talk about His human nature, and one last time to put it all together, both natures in the one person of Jesus Christ, and what that means for you and me.

Jesus Is True God

Jesus is true God, existing from eternity, all knowing, all powerful, transcendent, without flaw or weakness or sinful inclination. Jesus not only does not err or sin but He *cannot* err or sin—He is utterly, absolutely, completely perfect in His very being.

It is impossible to make an intellectually honest and scholastically legitimate argument against the existence of a person named

Jesus of Nazareth (more on that in the next section). Yet even with the acknowledgment that there was a person named Jesus of Nazareth, if He was just a man, His existence wouldn't make much of a difference for us. What is significant for us and for all of human history is that Jesus is God.

Before we go any further, though, we need to take a step back. What does it mean to be God? Who—or what—is God? Maybe you've never asked yourself this question before. If you were raised Christian, especially, you have probably always taken it for granted that there is an entity called God who rules over the universe. But in order to understand who Jesus is, we need to understand what it means to confess that Jesus is God.

The universe can be sorted into two basic categories: things that are God and things that are not God. Things that are not God are also called creation—and the God who made them, the Creator. You, me, your family, your pets, your neighbor's rock collection, the plant you keep forgetting to water, the Horsehead Nebula, the nucleus of a hydrogen atom, and everything else you can see, hear, taste, smell, and touch—and a lot of things you can't, like gamma rays and the molten iron core of the earth and even angels—they all fall into the category of creation. It's a pretty broad category, but all creatures share these very important things in common: they are not self-sufficient, they are not eternal, and they are not limitless. All of creation is deeply dependent, temporal, and limited by space and time . . . and the law of gravity and the water cycle and cellular respiration and lots of other things. And we are all, whether we know it or not, whether we like it or not, absolutely dependent upon God, our Creator.

This dependence is our ultimate identity, the thing that defines us and will always define us, even when Jesus returns.[1]

A hierarchy exists among created things, though it might not be what you would expect. For example, some Christians speak as though angels, the heavenly messengers of God, are of greater worth or significance to God than human beings. This tendency sneaks in especially after a loved one has died, when people might say that their deceased family member or friend has been transformed into an angel and is now in a better place. To be sure, a transformation does occur at death—the soul is separated from the body, a phenomenon we will return to later—but people do not cease to be human beings and become angels like the cosmic equivalent of getting a promotion or leveling up in a video game. Humans are humans eternally (a topic we will consider more deeply in the fourth chapter), and that's a good thing. God created human beings as the crown of His visible creation (Genesis 1:26–28). Human beings, just by existing, are more significant and God-pleasing than dogs or trees or the ocean or the whole universe.

When God created our first parents, Adam and Eve, He imparted to them His image. Theologians sometimes refer to this as the *imago Dei* (im-AH-go day-EE), a Latin term that means "image of God." This is an important but complicated part of

1 You ought to notice that none of the things in this list are *bad.* Sin isn't on this list. This is a really important point, but one that we'll have to return to in the next chapter. Suffice it to say for now: when sin entered the universe at the fall, it defaced and polluted the nature of all created things. We cannot now, by our own reason or strength, choose or will to rectify the problem of sin, whether that is our desire to do evil or our sentence to harm, decay, and death. But this was never meant to be, and it will be done away with once and for all when Jesus returns in triumph, which we'll turn to in the fourth chapter of this book. What will remain, even when Jesus returns to remake the heavens and the earth, is our identity as created beings and our dependence on God.

our God-given identities. The Book of Genesis indicates that some part of the image of God was lost in the fall. We were no longer able to refrain from sin and perfectly love as God does. On the other hand, some part of the image of God does remain in us. Like God, we are self-reflective, meaning we are aware of ourselves and how we affect the people and things around us. We are also, even after the fall, moral beings, meaning that we recognize the difference between right and wrong. Even non-Christians generally strive not to hurt people if they can help it, especially not the people they love. We are also capable of living in lifelong, intentional relationships with one another, whether that is in marriage, motherhood, fatherhood, or friendship. Neither clouds, cells, caterpillars, nor any of the rest of creation has this identity. No matter how cute and affectionate your dog is, he is not capable of self-reflective, moral thought. But you are because God chose to impart His image to you.

The human person is of unimaginable worth to God—which is why Jesus became a man in order to save us from eternal separation from God.

In contrast to us, God is not created. He is the Creator, outside of time and space, sufficient in Himself, without need for any person or thing. This is a bare-bones definition of what it means to be God, and one that we can actually talk about with people who aren't Christians, like Muslims, Hindus, or even some of the Greek philosophers popular in Jesus' own day. For example, the Greek philosopher Aristotle (384–322 BC) spoke of a God that was superior to the Greek pantheon of Athena and Apollo and friends that you might be familiar with, a God that was transcendent and unchangeable. He called this God "the unmoved mover" because this God had created (or "moved") the universe into existence; the unmoved mover had set off the first domino in the chain, but he himself was not in the chain, and he wasn't even a domino. We can agree with Aristotle on this point, but there is still a lot more that needs to be said about God.

We can learn about God in two ways: (1) through nature and reason and (2) through the Bible. By looking around us, we know that God is ordered, because of the fixed rules by which the universe operates, like gravity or mathematics, or the patterns that show up in creation, like the Fibonacci sequence or anatomical similarities between different animals. We know also that God is just: His Law has been written on the hearts of all men (Romans 2:14–15) so that all civilizations have similar legal codes, outlawing murder, theft, and adultery. Additionally, when societies ignore these laws, either altering their legal codes or scorning their consciences, bad things generally follow. Time and time again, history shows us that after periods of moral decadence and unethical living, cultures are left vulnerable to hostile takeovers, from the sack of Rome by the Visigoths to the rise of Hitler in Germany. Our own bodies sometimes bear the punishments for our sin: consider, for example, how gout was historically a disease that affected nobility because of their overindulgence in wine and rich foods. Nature itself bears witness to the wrath of God against evil, from hurricanes and earthquakes to pandemics. If we only had nature to tell us about God, we would probably end up like a lot of pagans: believing that God is orderly and just but is also fickle, angry, and out to get us, and that He must be appeased at all costs.

But we don't just have nature to tell us who God is, and we don't believe in a god that must be appeased like the pagans do. In addition to this "natural" knowledge of God, that is, things we can figure out on our own from nature, we also have "revealed" knowledge of God, that is, knowledge that we *can't* figure out on our own but that is instead given to us, or revealed, by God. God reveals His full identity to us in His Word, the Bible. Maybe you have heard someone describe the Bible as an acronym for "Basic Instructions Before Leaving Earth." While true to a point—God does provide His moral law to us in Scripture—this description actually misses the purpose of the Law: to show we are sinners powerless to save ourselves. The purpose of the Bible is that it reveals to us God's identity, and, you guessed it, points us to Jesus.

The Bible tells us again and again that God is merciful. He is so merciful because His very nature is love: "God is love" the apostle John tells us (see 1 John 4:7–21). This doesn't mean that God is squishy feelings of affection or romantic feelings of attraction. Rather, "love is patient and kind; love does not envy or boast; it is not arrogant or rude. It does not insist on its own way; it is not irritable or resentful; it does not rejoice at wrongdoing, but rejoices with the truth. Love bears all things, believes all things, hopes all things, endures all things. Love never ends" (1 Corinthians 13:4–8). Maybe you have heard this verse in the context of a wedding or a funeral. To be sure, as Christians, we ought to strive to live our lives in this sort of love, especially toward our spouse, family, and friends. But we will always fall short. We can't meet this standard for love, a fact to which we will return in the next chapter. But if God is love, and these verses from Paul tell us what love is, then they are also telling us *who God is*, especially the Second Person of the Trinity, Jesus Christ, who is God *for us*, the physical embodiment of divine mercy here to save and redeem mankind.

But what does all of that mean? For one, this is a radically different understanding of God than our pagan friends like Aristotle have. "Pagans," used here to refer to people who are not Christian, simply do not have this way of viewing God, because they do not know the Bible or they reject what the Bible would teach them about God. We can't really see much of God's love and mercy if we just go off of fallen creation. We have some, sure: some might see love in a god creating worlds and men and critters. They may even see mercy in the cycles of nature, night relenting to day and winter relenting to springtime. But these are such general kinds of love and mercy; they don't really tell us anything about salvation or whether God cares about us as unique individuals. The dog-eat-dog world around us is more likely to make it seem like salvation is something earned by hard work rather than given freely as a loving gift from God.

But the Bible tells us that God loves us dearly, mercifully relents from His wrath, and cares for the individual. The psalmist writes that God formed him—and you and me and everybody else—lovingly and uniquely in his mother's womb (Psalm 139:13). Isaiah echoes this, referring to "the Lord, your Redeemer, who formed you from the womb" (Isaiah 44:24). God said to Moses—and says to all of us—"I know you by name" (Exodus 33:17). But He doesn't just know us—He also loves us so deeply that He has chosen to save us. God knows each of us intimately, knowing our thoughts, words, and deeds even before we think, speak, or do them (Psalm 139)—even all of our sins, public and secret—yet He chose us before creating the first atom in the universe (see

Ephesians 1:4). John 3:16, a favorite of Sunday School children everywhere, captures God's love perfectly: "For God so loved the world, that He gave His only Son, that whoever believes in Him should not perish but have eternal life." This sweet, glorious, freeing Good News is for everyone, and it comes to us through God's Son, Christ Jesus.

Before we finally get to talk about Jesus and His divinity, it is worth noting that sometimes Christians and non-Christians have a hard time with the overwhelming mercy of God. Some Christians emphasize that God is fair and just above all things, or that He is sovereign and powerful above all things, or that He is rational and orderly and logical above all things. Certainly, all of these are attributes of God. God is just, sovereign, and orderly. But as Lutherans, we believe and teach that God is first and foremost *merciful*. For example, it would have been just, sovereign, and orderly to wipe out all of humanity as soon as Adam and Eve bit into the forbidden fruit. They broke the only rule in the universe: they rejected God. But rather than destroying all of humanity, God decided, out of unfathomable love and mercy, to send His own Son to die in our place to save us from this sin and death. Isn't it unjust to let a guilty man off for his crime? Isn't it humiliating to welcome back a traitor and betrayer? Isn't it disorderly to take the deserved punishment away from sinners and put it on the only sinless man, who is also God Himself, instead?

Frankly, it doesn't make sense. We do not deserve the mercy that God pours out on us. But this is how God makes Himself known—His unfathomable and immeasurable mercy. God is love, a self-sacrificing love that will bear all things in order to redeem the object of that love: us. Therefore, Jesus, true God, true Love, poured out His divine power and mercy to heal, redeem, and save us. That outpouring can be hard for us to face—how could the Word that spoke the universe into existence pour out His blood on a hideous torture device? We will consider that in greater detail in the next chapter, but you are right to be overwhelmed. Your non-Christian friend has a reason to be confused by the faith you confess. It doesn't make sense. It is a divine mystery that God chose us, but that's part of who God is—a merciful mystery that we don't seek to rationalize or figure out but merely revel in, and we give thanks for the profound Love of God, Jesus.

Let's examine another important element of God's identity that ties in with love, a reality that is deeply significant to our understanding of Jesus. God exists as a Trinity—three divine persons, yet one God. We must be careful when we talk about the Trinity because we can easily slip into error. Additionally, it is one of the most misunderstood doctrines of our Christian faith by people outside of the Church, and a poorly chosen analogy can end up generating more confusion, doubt, and unbelief than simply admitting that we don't understand either.

For example, perhaps you have heard a well-meaning Christian say she believes in a "God who exists in three ways." Unfortunately, this idiom is dangerously close to a heresy known as modalism, which the Early Church condemned. Modalism teaches that God reveals Himself in three "modes"—as though God plays three roles or wears three masks: God as Creator, God as Savior, and God as Sanctifier. Lutherans and the overwhelming majority of other Christians, like Roman Catholics, Presbyterians, Baptists, and Anglicans, among others, reject modalism and analogies that sound like it, because it denies the biblical truth that God exists in three *distinct* persons. The Father, the Son, and the Holy

Spirit are distinct, unique persons, not roles or masks assumed and cast aside. This easy slip from a good-hearted but incorrect analogy into literal heresy means that we must be very careful with how we speak about the Trinity.

Here is what we *can't* say. As Christians, we *do not* say that we worship three Gods. This is spelled out in very clear language in the Athanasian Creed, the long creed we confess once a year on Trinity Sunday. It is so thorough, in fact, that the best we can do here is summarize it and put it into slightly more digestible language. The Father, the Son, and the Holy Spirit are all God, but they are united in being God, or, as the Early Church Fathers said, they share a single *divine essence*. But, it's not like there is one God who just puts on a Father, Son, or Holy Spirit mask when the situation calls for it. The Father is not the Son or the Holy Spirit; the Son is not the Father or the Holy Spirit; and the Holy Spirit is not the Father or the Son. Each is a distinct person with a distinct role. God the Father created the world. God the Son, Jesus, is the Word through which the world was made, and He became man (we'll get to that in a few pages); through Jesus, the world was saved. God the Holy Spirit points us to Jesus, creating faith and working in us sanctification.

If the Trinity is confusing to you, that's okay. It's confusing to everybody, even the Church Fathers and theologians who first wrote helpful things about the Trinity for the rest of us. It's confusing because a lot of God's identity is hidden to us creatures. A great deal of it is revealed, like we said earlier, either through nature or in the words of the Bible, but there is still a lot we don't know—and probably *can't* know. This is part of what it means to be God, after all: since God is not a creature, it wouldn't make much sense for Him to be readily understood through creaturely reason.

We can say this, though: the Trinity points us back to the fact that God is love. God exists as three persons, yes, but in perfect unity, perfect love. And from this perfect love, He also created the world and everything in it. From this perfect love, Jesus, the Son of God, became incarnate, died, and rose to save you. In perfect love, the Holy Spirit continues to stir up in you faith and good works.

Jesus, then, exists as the Second Person of this Trinity, sometimes called the Word or the Son. Jesus is not God's son in a biological sense—God the Father and God the Holy Spirit are pure spirit, meaning they do not have physical bodies. Those depictions you see of God the Father as an old, bearded man are not meant literally, but rather they help communicate the idea that He is the Father. Jesus, unlike the other two persons of the Trinity, has a human body.

Jesus existed as God the Son before the incarnation when He took on human flesh and was born of Mary. Jesus existed together with the Father and the Holy Spirit before the beginning of time and the creation of the earth, and He also appears throughout the Old Testament. Traditionally, the Church has referred to these appearances as the "preincarnate Christ" or "preincarnate Son." Typically, theologians across history have considered most instances in the Old Testament of "the angel of the LORD" to refer to Jesus before His incarnation. (The word *angel* means "messenger" in both Hebrew and Greek, and therefore does not necessarily mean the spirit-being dwelling with God in heaven that we normally think of when we hear the word.) For example, when an angel appeared to Hagar to comfort her in the desert, that was Jesus. When Jacob wrestled with someone, that was Jesus. The voice that spoke to Moses out of the burning bush was a visitation of the preincarnate Christ, as was the rock that brought forth living waters in the desert, which Paul references in 1 Corinthians 10:4.

But the divine Logos, the eternal Son, "did not count equality with God a thing to be grasped" (Philippians 2:6), and so He stepped forth from the halls of inscrutable eternity to take on human flesh—our form—in order to save us. But what does that mean, that God has a body now in Christ? To answer that, we'll first look at what it means that Jesus is also true man.

Jesus Is True Man

Jesus is true man, a first-century rabbi (or teacher) who traveled around the Roman province of Judea, amassed followers, made enemies with the political and religious elites, preached, taught, spoke, laughed, cried, ate, drank, slept, walked, and was ultimately arrested, tried, crucified, and killed on charges of blasphemy.

It is vital that we understand that Jesus is also a real man—fully human, a fellow brother and partaker in our flesh.

Now, lots of religions talk about people being gods. For example, some of the Roman emperors referred to themselves as a "son of god," though they were of course not referring to the Christian God, Yahweh, but rather one of the many from their pagan pantheon. The Romans also had mythological figures who were both god and man; however, these individuals were the result of relations between a god and a human, like Hercules the demigod, who was half-god, half-man. Jesus of Nazareth, the historical figure who is also the Second Person of the Trinity, *became* man in time. He wasn't a man who earned divine status, nor was He the product of relations between a person and God (Christ's miraculous conception occurred by the Holy Spirit in Mary's womb, not through typical reproduction). He is the coeternal Second Person of the Trinity, who, at this moment in time, took on human flesh, fully.

Jesus was likely born around the year 4 BC (which is a little confusing—sorry, but the people who first came up with BC and AD were a little off on their math!) and was crucified around AD 30. Jesus' mother was a young woman, likely a teenager, named Mary. Mary, engaged to marry a man named Joseph, was visited by an angel, Gabriel, who told her she would miraculously conceive a baby by the work of the Holy Spirit (more on that later), despite being a virgin (Luke 1:26–28). An angel also appeared to Joseph, telling him not to divorce Mary because the baby in her womb had been conceived by the Holy Spirit, not a man, and is the prophesied messiah and "will save His people from their sins" (Matthew 1:18–25). Both Mary and Joseph were descended from King David. Some theologians believe this accounts for the discrepancies between the genealogies given at the beginning of the Gospels of Matthew and Luke. Thus, even on Jesus' adopted father's side, He is still the "shoot from the stump of Jesse" (Isaiah 11:1) and Son of David.

When Jesus was born, He was probably a lot like other babies. With ten tiny little fingers and ten toes, a big head that He wouldn't be able to keep upright on His own for months, and a body about the size of a loaf of bread, this is how the Word of God, who spoke the universe into existence from nothing, entered into our world: small, helpless, reliant on His mother to feed, bathe, dress, and otherwise care for Him.

Most of Jesus' life between His birth and the beginning of His ministry at age 30 is a bit of a blur. The Bible gives us a few stories—the Magi appearing while Jesus was a toddler (Matthew 2:1–12), the subsequent flight into Egypt to escape Herod (Matthew 2:13–18), the family's return to Judea (Matthew 2:19–23), the youth Jesus in the temple (Luke 2:41–52). Many of these accounts are significant because they fulfill Old Testament prophecies. For example, Jesus' birth to the Virgin Mary at Bethlehem fulfills prophecies from Genesis 3:15, Isaiah 7:14, and Micah 5:2. Those genealogies at the beginning of Matthew and Luke show that Jesus fulfilled at least a half dozen prophecies throughout the Old Testament foretelling the Messiah's lineage (see Genesis 12:3; 17:19; 21:12; 22:18; 49:10; Numbers 24:17; 2 Samuel 7:12–13; Isaiah 9:7). Hosea's words "out of Egypt I called My son" (11:1) ring true at the flight to and return from Egypt; and even the slaughter of the innocents, when King Herod ordered all the infant male children killed in an attempt to halt the coming Messiah (Matthew 2:16–18), was predicted: "A voice is heard in Ramah, lamentation and bitter weeping. Rachel is weeping for her children; she refuses to be comforted for her children, because they are no more" (Jeremiah 31:15). Additionally, these experiences all underscore the humanness of our Lord. Jesus is fully human, which means He experienced all of what it means to be human, including the experience of being born and growing up, developing physically and mentally, growing taller and stronger, sleeping, waking, becoming hungry, getting hurt, falling ill, feeling lonely.

Sometimes, we have a tendency to think of being human as a sort of punishment in and of itself. How many times have you heard someone say they were "only human," for example? Or have you ever been told that, after death, Christians become angels? Both of these sentiments confuse the nature of what it means to be human, and as a result, obscure Jesus' true identity and our own.

Human beings are sinful as a result of the fall. This truth is found again and again in the Bible and is readily apparent in our lives and throughout history. A key part of what it means to be human has been fundamentally changed as a result of the fall: mankind is now enslaved to sin and death. We cannot right our relationship with God by our own strength or merit, and we are now open to pain, harm, illness, decay, and ultimately, death.

Jesus likewise suffered as we do. Traditionally, theologians refer to this as Christ's "humiliation." After all, why would God, who created and rules all things, allow Himself to suffer, whether that's experiencing hunger or death on a cross? Some other religious groups, such as Muslims, view the Christian belief that God became man in Christ as deeply offensive for this very reason—and, though it may push against our reason, we view His incarnation in wonder! It is utterly baffling that the God who spoke the stars into existence would take on mortal, physical flesh so that He would have to experience all of the limitations of our human bodies, ultimately culminating in being tortured to death.

But this is the other vital part of what it means to be human: despite our fall into sin, being human is still good. Why? Because God says it is in the person of Jesus.

Yes, you are sinful by nature and you sin in thought, word, and deed. But, nevertheless, the almighty Lord of heaven and earth saw fit to bring together the sperm and egg that first sparked with your life. He made you, a human, male or female, as a person who has intrinsic worth as a creature made by the God who gives things their worth. He didn't make you a rock or a bug or a bear—though those are also good things created by God. No, He made you a human person, the crown of creation, to look after all the rocks and bugs and bears and everything else.

Sometimes, we forget that, despite the fall, creation is still good—being *human* is still good. We are no longer sinless, and creation has become horribly warped by the sin that has flourished, but both creation and humanity are *still* good because God has redeemed us and will restore all creation.

God taking on human flesh in the person of Jesus is the ultimate affirmation of the goodness of being human, because your Savior, your God, is your Brother—your fully human Brother.

Jesus' humanity also means that He is a historical figure. This doesn't mean He was *merely* a historical figure, but it does mean that Jesus has a verifiable historical record, a claim not many other religions can make. Many religions are completely ahistorical, meaning that their deities have little to no historically verifiable interactions with mankind. Most indigenous religions, as well as reconstructed neo-pagan religions like Wicca and certain occultist groups, have no historical record of the deities they believe in intervening with the physical world. To put it another way, a Wiccan would not—and, moreover, *could* not—say that someone claiming to be the Triple Goddess walked around England in the 1950s, gained followers, and was seen performing miracles. If you could find someone who practices Aztec religion, they would not and could not claim that the rain god, Quetzalcòatl, gave prophecies about future events that proved to be true. Even religions that involve historically verifiable figures, such as Buddhism and its founder, Siddhartha Gautama, or Islam and its prophet, Muhammad, struggle to claim the same factual status. For example, the birth and death dates for the Siddhartha Gautama, the first Buddha, differ by as much as two hundred years, and there is little definitive historical information available about his life. While we have more details about the life of Muhammad, his interactions with the angel with whom he claimed to have spoken are unverifiable as there were no witnesses, and there are few historical records of his life that predate the Qur'an, which itself does not give a narrative of Muhammad's life.

The Bible, while obviously our sacred religious text, does provide a historically verifiable account of the human man known as Jesus of Nazareth. Unlike other religious texts, like the Qur'an in Islam or the Vedic texts of Hinduism, the Old and New Testaments both reference specific historical figures and realities, such as rulers, geographic locations, and international power dynamics—references that can be cross-checked and verified, and which have been. For example, we know that Jesus was born while Augustus was emperor and was crucified when Pontius Pilate was governor of the Roman providence of Judea. Using this information from the Bible, we can find corresponding historical records to verify the claims the Bible makes.

In addition to the words of Scripture, we also have a number of historical records that prove to us that Jesus was a real person and that the Bible gives a reliable account of His life. Now, of course, because Jesus lived about two thousand years ago, we don't have the typical documentation that you might be thinking of—no birth certificate, government-issued identification, medical records, or anything like that. The only official historical records (or at least the only sources that have survived two millennia of time passing and material decaying!) are government records, usually in the form of edicts, letters from officials, or government-sponsored written histories. An unofficial historical record exists, too, some of which has survived and some of which has not. This includes poems and songs, wall paintings (called frescoes), and graffiti.

These documents verify the reality of Jesus of Nazareth, a Jew living in the Roman Empire during the reigns of Augustus and later Tiberius, who claimed to be the Messiah and whose story is told in the New Testament. In fact, we actually have better evidence to support the existence of a real Jesus of Nazareth, a Hellenic Jew who claimed to be God and gained a following first in the rural backwaters and then some of the urban centers of the Roman Empire, than we have to support the existence and authentic authorship of historical figures like Aristotle. The Roman historian Tacitus, for example, talks about the followers of someone named "Christus," who lived during the reign of the emperor Tiberius and procuratorship of Pontius Pilate. These followers of Christ were ruthlessly persecuted by then-emperor Nero, Tacitus reports, under the guise that their superstitious beliefs and antisocial lifestyle had, somehow, caused the destructive fires of the city of Rome (Tacitus, *Annales* 44.2–5). This source is one of the most famous pieces of evidence for the historical reality of Jesus of Nazareth because it also shows that His followers were willing to die for their beliefs; Nero, after pinning the fires of Rome on the Christians, publicly tortured and executed them in an attempt to win favor with the Roman people.

Jesus shows up in other ancient sources as well. The governor Pliny wrote Trajan, the emperor, asking for advice on how to handle the new Christian problem: Christians, of course, would not sacrifice in pagan temples or worship Roman gods, which were major requirements of Roman civic duty. Lack of proper reverence, the Romans feared, could lose them their favor with the gods. Christians were being accused of "superstition" because of their unwillingness to join in proper Roman religious observances and festivals, and some were being brought to the governor for punishment (Pliny, *Letters* 10.96).

Of course, it isn't enough to believe that Jesus was a historical figure. We aren't called upon to confess Jesus as an itinerant Jewish preacher who found Himself at odds with the religious establishment in first-century Judea. We are called upon to confess Jesus as Christ—as a historical figure, a true man, but also God Himself in the flesh, because "if you confess with your mouth that Jesus is Lord and believe in your heart that God raised Him from the dead, you will be saved" (Romans 10:9). Nevertheless, our Lord and Savior Jesus Christ *was* and still *is* a historical figure, a real human being who left a historical record of His existence. Not only that, but He took on His incarnate identity—His real experience of being human, His being born and living and breathing and eating and sleeping and, yes, even dying—all for us, so that He might redeem our fallen bodies through His perfect one.

Your God became a man for you, and He continues to be a man even now, so that He will eternally be your neighbor, your brother, your friend.

Jesus Is True God and True Man

To fully know Jesus is to know Him as both God and man.

God has given us the Scriptures in order that we might know Jesus fully: Jesus as both man and God, the Christ, Son of the living God. The pages of the Bible all point forward (the Old Testament) or backward (the New Testament) to the incarnate God-man, Jesus, true God who became true man in order to redeem us body and soul. The incarnation is central to our identity as Christians for this reason: without it, nothing else that Christ does makes any sense.

But in order to understand the incarnation, we have to be incredibly careful not to mix up Jesus' identity as both God and man, while also understanding how those two natures—the human nature and the divine nature—interact. There isn't a "human Jesus" and a "God Jesus," then, but rather one Jesus, who possesses both a human nature and a divine nature. The Lutheran theologian Martin Chemnitz, who has been called the "Second Martin" because of his importance in leading the Lutheran Church after the death of Martin Luther, helped lay out how these two parts of Jesus' identity work—and what it means for us—in response to a number of theological controversies that cropped up in the Reformation. Chemnitz and other theologians wrote a document called the Formula of Concord, a comprehensive overview of how Lutherans understand the Bible on a number of topics, from free will to Jesus' descent into hell. The Formula of Concord has the following to say about Jesus' human and divine natures:

> We believe, teach, and confess that God's Son from eternity has been a particular, distinct, entire, divine person. Yet He is true, essential, perfect God with the Father and the Holy Spirit. In the fullness of time He received also the human nature into the unity of His person. He did not do this in such a way that there are now two persons or two Christs. Christ Jesus is now in one person at the same time true, eternal God, born of the Father from eternity, and a true man, born of the most blessed Virgin Mary. This is written in Romans 9:5, "from their race, according to the flesh, is the Christ who is God over all, blessed forever."
>
> We believe, teach, and confess that now, in this one undivided person of Christ, there are two distinct natures: the divine, which is from eternity,

and the human, which in time was received into the unity of the person of God's Son. These two natures in the person of Christ are never either separated from or mingled with each other. Nor are they changed into each other. Each one abides in its nature and essence in the person of Christ to all eternity.

We believe, teach, and confess also that both natures mentioned remain unmingled and undestroyed in their nature and essence. Each keeps its natural, essential properties to all eternity and does not lay them aside. Neither do the essential properties of the one nature ever become the essential properties of the other nature. (Formula of Concord, Solid Declaration, Article 8, paragraphs 6–8)

So let's go through all of that. The Son of God has been God from before the beginning of time when He existed in Trinity with the Father and the Holy Spirit, the three of whom are nevertheless bound in perfect unity as the one and only true God. Jesus, this same Son of God, took on human flesh when He was conceived and born of the Virgin Mary, but this isn't a new Jesus or a new God. Rather, Jesus is both the true Son of God from all eternity *and* the Son of Mary, fully human with human features and a historical record. Jesus has both a *divine* nature and a *human* nature, but He is one unified person, and those two natures don't get all muddled and mixed up into a new, "divine-ish/human-ish" nature or "god-ish/man-ish" person.

Now, by "human nature," we don't mean an inclination to sin. Sometimes, we use the phrase "I am only human" to express our sinful tendencies and failings. In those cases, we use the term "human nature" when we really mean "concupiscence," or the inward inclination felt by all human beings (save one, Christ Jesus) after the fall into sin. It is ultimately this *desire* to sin, or our sinful nature, that separates us from God and gives rise to the individual sins we commit. Hypothetically speaking, a person could refrain from outwardly sinning. In fact, to an extent, you probably have yourself; in all likelihood, you've never robbed a bank, killed someone, or worshiped a golden idol. But even if you had, the reason why you commit any sin is because of the disordered state of your soul: your—and my—sinful nature desires hateful things and hates desirable things. The good we wish to do we do not, and the evil we wish not to do we keep on doing (see Romans 7:19–25).

But Christ took on our human nature—not our sin nature, as He is God and without sin—our finite bodies with constant material needs and incessant weaknesses. Jesus, the Son of God, with God from before the beginning of all creation, has always had a divine nature, but at the incarnation, when the Holy Spirit overshadowed Mary and brought about the miraculous conception of Jesus, He also took on a human nature.

Elsewhere, Martin Chemnitz uses the term "the communication of attributes" to describe how Jesus could have two natures simultaneously. The short and simple version: in many ways, we will never fully know how Jesus could be both God and man at the same time. He is, after all, God, and a key part of what it means to be God is being transcendent, or above our understanding. But at another level, it is important that we don't misunderstand what we do know about the life and work of Jesus. We will discuss this more in the fourth chapter, but it's worth talking about here too. For much of Jesus' ministry, especially before the crucifixion, He "hid" His divine nature; the devil himself tempted Christ to make use of His divinity by making stones into bread, for example, which Jesus refused to do. In the very crucifixion, Jesus allowed Himself to die, which is certainly the pinnacle of laying His almighty power aside for our sake. At other times, however, He makes use of His divine nature, like when He performs miracles or when He appears in the locked upper room after the resurrection.

This might seem like a contradiction—how can a man do these things? Remember, Jesus isn't a demigod like Hercules, and He isn't some third category of "God-man" where He's fifty-fifty God and man, like a labradoodle is half Labrador, half poodle. Jesus is 100 percent true God and 100 percent true man, simultaneously. And so, even though Jesus as true man shouldn't be able to calm the seas, materialize out of thin air, heal the sick, raise the dead, turn water into wine, or any of the other miracles contained within the Gospel accounts, He nevertheless *can* do them because He is also true God. These abilities and attributes that Jesus has as God are "communicated," or shared, with the human nature, so that Jesus, still fully man, can do things that break the laws of nature.

So let's put it all together: In the beginning was the Word (the Son of God, Second Person of the Trinity) who was with God (with the Father and the Holy Spirit in the mystery of the Trinity) and who was God (all three equal to each other with respect to divine identity, or omnipotence, omnipresence, omniscience, uncreatedness, self-sufficiency, and loving mercy). But all three are separate and distinct as persons (not masks or roles or forces, but the Father, Son, and Holy Spirit each existing in and of themselves), yet also existing in unity as one God (not three Gods or three Lords, but one God, one Lord). This Word, Jesus Christ, was with God from the beginning before time, and it is through Him that the whole world was made. This Word took on our human frame—became flesh—and dwelt among us, in order that He might redeem us from our sin. The Holy Spirit caused Mary, despite being a virgin, to miraculously conceive Jesus in her womb, and in that moment, God became man.

Jesus is fully God and fully man in a way we can't understand, having the full and actual body, organs, thoughts, feelings, and soul like all men, but also having the power and wisdom and glory and might of God.

Fully man and fully God, Jesus became a human being in order to save you.

He was born, named, circumcised, and presented in the temple for you. He fled into Egypt and returned to Nazareth for you. He grew in wisdom and stature and sat at the feet of the teachers of the temple for you. He was baptized for you. He was tempted for you. He called the Twelve, turned water into wine, cleansed the temple, instructed Nicodemus, baptized, taught, healed the sick, raised the dead, preached, cast out demons, ate with tax collectors and sinners, gave parables, transfigured, and foretold His death and resurrection for you. He triumphantly entered Jerusalem for you. He instituted the Lord's Supper at the Passover for you. He was captured, beaten, mocked, interrogated, humiliated, tortured for you. He carried His cross for you. He was nailed to the cross for you, forgave the thief on the cross for you, pleaded to the Father for you, gave up His last breath for you, was pierced in His side for you. He was buried for you. He rested in the tomb on the Sabbath for you. And He rose from the dead for you, appeared to the women and to the disciples for you, comforted the men on the road to Emmaus, and took away Thomas's doubts for you. He ascended into heaven for you, where He sits at the right hand of the Father for you. He will come back for you, and He is always interceding for you before the Father.

Jesus is God and man because that is how He is able to be our Savior. Because He is God, He can conquer sin and death as a guiltless, perfect sacrifice. Because He is man, He can take your place as your true Brother. Jesus is God and man for you.

Jesus Is True God and True Man for You

So what does Christ's incarnation tell us about our identity, about our own bodies and humanity?

Oftentimes, people swing between the extremes of ultimate self-infatuation and intense self-hatred. Both are sinful, and both are corrected through the incarnation of Christ and atoned for through His death and resurrection.

We sometimes act as though we have absolute control over ourselves, our bodies, and our circumstances in life. When we place ourselves at this pinnacle, in this godlike status, we quickly spin out of control, desecrating our bodies, misusing creation, and harming people around us. Individuals may seek this control through misguided medical interventions meant to alter an individual's God-given sex or through occult practices that promise knowledge of the future or influence over one's romantic or economic situation. While these are extreme examples, all of us delude ourselves into thinking that we have greater control over our lives than we do. Most of us live the majority of our lives cushioned from the reality that God alone is master over creation, and this impacts the way that we treat ourselves and those around us. We treat creation like a worthless possession rather than a priceless treasure over which we have been placed as stewards. We treat other people like dolls to play with and discard at our own leisure, not as fellow bearers of the holy image of God. We treat our bodies like they are temporary and meaningless puppets, when in reality our bodies are the mysterious and beloved temples of the Holy Spirit which God continues to proclaim as good.

On the flip side, we can be driven to pits of self-loathing, directed either at all of humanity or our individual selves. While there are certain relatively obscure eco-terrorist groups that literally want to end the human existence in favor of plants and animals, those people are relatively few and far between. Far more common is that pervasive misanthropy that so many of us have fallen into, the sweeping unkind generalizations we make about huge groups of people, the lack of concern for the people with whom we interact on a daily basis, the growing sense of total despair that so many of us feel when we read or watch the news. And there's the problem of self-hatred, whether it's the callous way many of us think, speak, and act toward ourselves or, in some extreme cases, individuals struggling with self-harm or suicidal ideations. These feelings can be especially strong when we feel disconnected from our bodies, when we struggle against the limitations that are natural to all human beings. Frustrated with our being bound in time and space, our frailty, our dependence on the cycles of nature, let alone those consequences of the fall like sickness and death, we can despair of being human, even being alive altogether. Throw in our inability to free ourselves from our sinful nature (more on that in the next chapter), and the picture looks rather bleak.

Are we the source of all worth, or are we worthless? Are we each a god unto ourselves, or are we all irredeemable devils?

Neither. And that's what we can learn from Jesus' incarnation.

Jesus is God. You are not. This reorientation is crucial to understanding our place within the universe.

It can be so tempting and seemingly desirable to set ourselves up as divine—that is how Satan tempted Adam and Eve, after all! But this desire will only leave us overwhelmed, confused, and empty. This will drive us to sin and ultimately to despair, even death. And this is why Jesus, the true Son of God, the eternal, all-knowing, all-capable Word, came to save you. Because you couldn't do it yourself. Because you are a dear and beloved *child* of God, a cherished *creation*, not a creator. Jesus, true God, comes to put you back into your place.

But your place is also as a precious brother or sister of Christ. Because the very Son of God has taken on human flesh—your flesh—your body has been redeemed. Humanity, every single human being, has been saved through Christ taking on our form and dying to save us. God looks at you through Christ and proclaims you to be very good, your soul and your body redeemed, made perfect, restored.

Restored by Jesus, freed from the delusion of thinking that we are god and comforted of the despair that we are devoid of worth, we are then set loose to share this with our neighbor and to let Jesus redefine our identity. You do not need to search for meaning in the passing things of this world or war against the created order because God has made you as His creation. Your life is not a mistake and you are not worthless because God Himself became a man to save you. And that God-man is Jesus, whom you get to share with the rest of the world.

Who is this Jesus? Jesus is King. Jesus is Lord. Jesus is the Prince of Peace. Jesus is love. Jesus is the answer. Jesus is God. Jesus is man. Jesus is the door. Jesus is the bread of life. Jesus is your Savior. Yours! For you!

In Matthew 16:13–20, Jesus asks His disciples who they think He is. Peter answers, "You are the Christ, the Son of the living God!" (v. 16). Jesus asks us this same question but not as a sort of pop quiz or comprehension test. Rather, this question and its answer are to give us comfort. By faith, we cling to the mind-blowing mystery of the incarnation, which was accomplished *for us*! The Lord of Life, by whom the entire universe was created—from galaxies to gamma rays and everything in between—stepped out from the halls of eternity and took on flesh, taking on the humble form of a developing baby in the womb of Mary. Jesus, who was present at the creation of light, of space, of time, laid aside His universe-making power and omnipotence so that He might remake the universe—so that He might remake *you*, redeem *you*, save *you*.

Our God cares so much about our bodies and bodily well-being that He Himself took on a body so that all bodies might be renewed.

Who is Jesus? Jesus is our true God, who took on real human flesh as true man in order to save you and me.

CHAPTER ONE STUDY QUESTIONS

1. We talked a lot in this chapter about how Jesus has two natures but is one person. Using the examples and definitions on pages 18 and 19, define ***nature*** and ***person*** in this context.

2. What are the two categories that divide the whole universe, and what differentiates them?

3. What can we find out about God from nature, reason, and the world around us? What can we find out about God ***only*** from the Bible?

4. Other religions talk about human beings who became gods or who were "sons of gods." How is Jesus different from these mythological figures?

5. What can we learn about Jesus from the Bible? What can we learn about Jesus from history? What purpose do these two types of knowledge serve?

6. Look back on page 32 for the (incomplete!) list of Old Testament prophecies and their fulfillment in the life of Christ. If you are in a group, give each person a verse or two to look up; if reading individually, pick a few that are of particular interest to you. What strikes you about these passages? What is the

significance of the little tidbits from the early life of Christ?

7. **What does it mean that Jesus has two natures but one person?**

8. **What are some of the ways that we get our human identities wrong?**

9. **What does the incarnation tell us about our identity?**

10. **Who is Jesus? Why is this important?**

CHAPTER TWO

WHAT DID JESUS DO?

In the last chapter, we discussed how Jesus is both true God and true man, who has existed since before time as God but who took on a human body within time so that He could save us. But how did He save us? What did He do? That's what we'll be considering in this chapter.

What did Jesus do? Well, Jesus did a lot of things. He performed miracles, gave sermons, spoke in parables. He was born and grew up. He ate, drank, and slept. He laughed. He cried. He proclaimed things that we should and shouldn't do. He offered an example for how we should live our own lives. All of these things are things Jesus did, but there's something else too: Jesus died.

Even if you've been a Lutheran your whole life, there's always something a little shocking about saying (or reading) those words.

Jesus died. And Jesus didn't just die. Jesus was tortured to death.

I once took a day trip to a Catholic monastery and shrine with my husband (at the time, my fiancé) and our pastor, who wanted to take us there because of their Stations of the Cross. If you've never seen or participated in the Stations of the Cross, it's a set of twelve to fourteen scenes, or "stations," from the Passion narrative, leading up to the crucifixion. Sometimes, churches will do a live one with people posing (called a tableau), or they will have paintings, carvings, or sculptures up year-round or as part of a Holy Week service or activity. The shrine had beautiful carvings, but the real focus was the crucifix at the end. Our pastor told us not to peek, so we didn't, and we were shocked when we got to the end: suspended on the wall, about twenty feet up in the air, was one of the largest crucifixes I've ever seen—it was larger than life-sized—and also one of the bloodiest. We all burst into tears at the sight of it.

Sometimes, the empty cross, and even some crucifixes, can give us the sense that Jesus' death was peaceful. This was anything but. The Christ on this cross was covered in blood, gasping for breath, and utterly crushed, just like the prophet Isaiah describes in Isaiah 53. It was heartrending; it was downright upsetting. And yet, that's exactly what happened. That's exactly what Christ did: Jesus died.

But that's also not all Jesus did. Jesus also rose from the dead! A joy beyond all comprehension! A miracle above all miracles! The unutterable horror of God dying is undone by the unspeakable awe and gladness of that very God defeating death itself—and not for His own sake but for all of us!

This is why, despite the fact that Jesus did many things in the Gospels, we focus on His suffering on the cross, or His death and resurrection. Jesus' crucifixion is the literary climax of each of the four Gospel accounts. It's what the apostles preach in the Book of Acts, and it's the resounding focus of the Epistles written to the early churches. Even the Book of Revelation, which we will turn to in greater detail in the fourth chapter, is focused on what Jesus accomplished on the cross.

Additionally, Christ's crucifixion is foretold throughout the Old Testament. From the words of comfort God speaks to Adam and Eve after the fall in Genesis 3:15, sometimes referred to as the protoevangelium, or "first Gospel," to the Twenty-Second Psalm, which Jesus recites from the cross, to the Suffering Servant in the Book of Isaiah, Jesus' crucifixion is even the focus of the *Old* Testament! Our forefathers in the faith didn't know that they were waiting on a Galilean carpenter named Jesus to be killed on a

Roman cross, but they did know that God was going to provide a sacrifice of Himself in order to rectify the sin and death we had brought into the world. God was in the business of making covenants, or promises, to save and redeem His people, covenants that rested fully on Him, where He took the full burden of the promise and the sacrifice, despite everything being our fault.

Jesus' crucifixion was the fulfillment of the covenants in the Old Testament, the long-awaited sacrifice that would finally put to right what had been broken in Eden and ever since.

Furthermore, the crucifixion is what makes Jesus, well, Jesus. The crucifixion and resurrection shows us that Jesus isn't a prophet, or a healer, or a magician, or a wise man, or a respectable teacher, or a conman. The crucifixion is what makes Jesus the Christ: *Christ* is the Greek translation of the Hebrew word *Messiah*, or *savior*. *Christ* literally means "anointed one."

Why is Jesus the Anointed One? In the Old Testament, kings, who defended and ruled their people, and high priests, who made the sacrifices in the temple, were typically anointed, as the act of anointing set them apart from others to fulfill a task given to them by God. The two roles were united in Jesus, who is our King and our High Priest, ruler of the universe, and yet sacrificing Himself before God on our behalf to grant us mercy and forgiveness of our sins.

Jesus became the Anointed One in His Baptism, when He was anointed with the Holy Spirit (see Acts 10:38). Additionally,

Jesus is "set apart," both as unique in His two natures as God and man, as we talked about in the last chapter, and also as a sacrifice, set apart like a Passover lamb, without spot or blemish. But this sacrifice is itself different and special, as it is the once-for-all sacrifice for all mankind. *Messiah* also means "savior" or "redeemer," or even "liberator."

But Jesus didn't come to save, redeem, or liberate us from a political regime or even gross societal injustice, as the Jewish leaders and even some of His followers believed. Instead, Jesus saves, redeems, and liberates us from the tyranny of sin and death. At His crucifixion, Jesus is anointed in His own holy, innocent blood. He, in turn, anoints us so that we may be forgiven our sins; given the desire and, through the Holy Spirit, the ability to live in accordance with the Law of God; and ultimately freed even from the shackles of death, the just punishment for our sin (see Romans 6:3–4). Through His death, Jesus takes your place and gives you His own, where you are anointed, set apart, and washed clean of your sin so you appear before the Father not in the dirty, bloody, foul trappings of your sin—which Jesus took onto Himself—but rather in Jesus' sinlessness and blessedness.

What did Jesus do? Jesus died for you. Jesus rose from the dead for you too.

Jesus Died

In the previous chapter, we discussed how big of a deal it was that God became man in the person of Jesus Christ. So why did Jesus, after going to all the trouble of the incarnation, living on earth for thirty-three years, breathing, eating, sleeping, then decide to *die*? Why did Jesus have to die?

We can answer this question in a couple of ways. The first is to look at the immediate context of the crucifixion in the Bible. Jesus was brought before Pilate by the Jewish leaders, who were accusing Him of blaspheming. Specifically, they were accusing Jesus of falsely claiming to be God. Now, they were partially right: Jesus did, in fact, claim to be God, as we talked about in the previous chapter. Though they are not always immediately recognizable to us now, many of Jesus' statements about Himself—"I am the Good Shepherd" (John 10:11); "I and the Father are one" (John 10:30); "Before Abraham was, I am" (John 8:58)—were direct, bold claims of divinity. The issue was that the scribes and Jewish leaders did not believe Jesus; they did not think that He was the promised Messiah, the fulfillment of the prophecies of the Old Testament, the very Son of God, come to redeem the world.

But how is this possible? How could God's own people not recognize Him bodily in their midst?

Jesus' audience had the Old Testament Scriptures, but they rejected the good news that God was sending the Messiah to save them from their sins. The two main Jewish groups with whom Jesus interacted were the Pharisees (often associated with the scribes) and the Sadducees (associated with the priestly class running the temple). Both groups had at least part of the Scriptures, yet they both rejected Christ. The Sadducees only held sacred the first five books of the Bible, believing the rest of the Old Testament to be illegitimate, and they also rejected any doctrine about the immortality of the soul and the resurrection of the dead. On the other hand, the Pharisees did read the entire Old Testament, but they also held to something called the "oral law" or "oral Torah," a series of laws not recorded in the Old Testament that had to do with everything from what you could and couldn't do on the Sabbath to washing your hands around mealtime. While the Sadducees rejected Christ because they rejected the reality of the resurrection, and thus a need for salvation and the hope for eternal life, the Pharisees rejected Him because they relied on their own good works in following the oral traditions, rules which Jesus and His disciples did not always obey since they were not scriptural. On account of both of these groups, Jesus said, "You search the Scriptures because you think that in them you have eternal life; and it is they that bear witness about Me, yet you refuse to come to Me that you may have life" (John 5:39–40).

The connection between the ancient tribes of Israel and the modern nation-state of Israel, or the faith of the patriarchs and prophets of the Old Testament and that of contemporary Jews who claim continuity with them, may be confusing. It is important to make clear that modern Judaism rejects Jesus as the Messiah. (There is an exception, of course, in Messianic Judaism, which holds that Jesus is the Christ; Messianic Jews are Christians who have retained much of the liturgical and cultural heritage of Judaism.) Jews are not Christian because they have rejected Christ. Additionally, the modern country of Israel is *not* the Israel spoken of in many of the prophecies of the Old and New Testaments. The Biblical Israel is rather a way of speaking about the people of God across time, including His chosen people in the Old Testament. (We will return to this in more detail in the fourth chapter.)

So if Jesus was killed because He claimed to be God, why did He need to do that—and why did He allow Himself to be killed in the first place? If we zoom out a bit from the immediate context surrounding the crucifixion, we see that Jesus died to take away the punishment we deserve for our sin.

We first need to back up to the very beginning to figure out what sin is and why it has such intense repercussions. When God warned Adam not to eat the fruit of the tree of the knowledge of good and evil, He said that on the day Adam ate of it, he would surely die (Genesis 2:17). This can be a bit difficult for us to fully understand because death so deeply permeates our experience now—death is something we have to learn to understand and respond to as children, whether because of the death of a friend or family member or even just the death of a beloved household pet. We say things like "death is natural" or "death is a part of life"—but it ought not be, and it wasn't originally. Adam had no experience of death when God gave this warning because death is a complete undoing of God's good creative work. As we discussed in the previous chapter, God created man to be body and soul, united in one person. At death, the body and soul are violently torn asunder. Death is not just an end of biological functioning; it is totally antithetical to what it means to be human in that it strips the God-breathed soul from its body.

But as horrible as death is, it's really only a symptom of the underlying problem: a rejection of God.

Just like death rips apart the human body and soul, sin tears us away from God because it destroys the relationship of trusting dependence and loving faith that was present between Adam and Eve and the Lord in the garden.

Adam and Eve sinned by rejecting the Word of God that was attached to the tree. We'll talk in the next chapter about sacraments, the physical means to which Jesus has attached His Word and Himself in order to give us salvation. We can use this way of thinking to also help us understand the fall and why taking a piece of fruit is such a cosmically big deal. In a way, the tree of the knowledge of good and evil was also sort of like a sacrament: God had attached His Word—though this time it was a word of warning—to a physical thing, the fruit of this tree. By trusting this word and acting—or *not* acting—in accordance with it, Adam and Eve received God's good gifts—union and harmony with the triune Godhead—by faith. When they ignored this word and took of the fruit, they were putting themselves in the place of God, desecrating a holy thing and destroying their relationship with God in the process.

Every individual sin and the general state of being in sin, a state into which we are all born as a result of the fall, is always a rejection of God, and it is always destructive. Across the centuries, theologians have stressed that sin is so absolutely destructive that it isn't really even a "thing." The Bible tells us that God created everything in the universe (Colossians 1:16) but also that God did *not* create sin (1 John 1:5; James 1:13), which seems to be a bit of a paradox. But sin is actually an absence: an absence of trust in God, an absence of love for neighbor, an absence of the capacity to choose to have faith in God or to do good. Think of it this way: evil people, throughout history or in our personal lives, are always *destroying* things, whether that's the beauty of God's creation, expressions of truth, institutions and groups doing good, or, ultimately, human life itself. The most frightening villains in literature and culture, from Mephistopheles in Goethe's *Faust*, to Sauron in J. R. R. Tolkien's *The Lord of the Rings*, to Thanos in the Marvel Cinematic Universe, are always sowing destruction because they are embodiments of this destructive, sinful state in which we find ourselves. We are trapped in this sinful void, which the Bible describes again and again as darkness, where the light of God's love cannot be found.

Except for when that Light, Jesus Christ Himself, broke into the darkness in order to destroy it once and for all.

But how do you destroy evil itself? How do you undo the great undoing of our right relationship with God, with one another, and with the whole universe? Again, let's go back to the beginning. When God finds Adam and Eve, they are attempting to cover their nakedness—they are trying to hide their wrongdoing and their shame. But they can't. Somewhat surprisingly, God kills an animal and, taking its skin, clothes Adam and Eve with that instead. God performs the first sacrifice to atone for sin in Genesis 3:21, with this death happening in order to avert the deserved death of Adam and Eve. Adam and Eve will still die, but this is a sign that they will not die eternally—that is, they will not be damned to hell for eternity.

This pattern of sacrifice continued throughout the Old Testament. The patriarchs were always offering sacrifices, and oftentimes, God intervened and offered His own, like the covenant with Abraham (Genesis 15:1–15) and the ram in the thicket taking Isaac's place on the sacrificial pyre (Genesis 22). The sacrificial system was put into place and regulated through Moses, with Aaron set up as the first high priest (Exodus 28:1), and it continued under kings David and Solomon (2 Chronicles 5:1–10). When Israel split into two kingdoms—the Northern Kingdom (Israel) and the Southern Kingdom (Judah)—the Southern Kingdom, where Jerusalem was located, continued the sacrificial system that God had given them. However, the Northern Kingdom set up new sacrifices in places and ways that God had forbidden (1 Kings 12:25–33), resulting in their ultimate judgment and destruction through the forced deportation of Israel by Assyria (1 Chronicles 5:26; 2 Kings 16:9, 15:29). This is the region that was known as Samaria in the New Testament, whose inhabitants were scorned by the Jews because of their unfaithfulness. Eventually, even the temple sacrifice system in Jerusalem came to an end, most clearly seen through the historical reality of the destruction of the temple in AD 70, predicted by Jesus Himself (Matthew 24:2).

This sacrificial system can sometimes be confusing to us. "But we don't offer anything to God!" we rightly say. And that's correct. We don't. And neither did they, at least they weren't *doing* something that *merited* salvation and mercy in and of itself. God repeatedly says throughout the Old Testament that He does not delight in these sacrifices, and He is displeased by sacrifices performed emptily, without a heart of faith (see Isaiah 29:13; Matthew 15:7–9; Hebrews 11:6). These sacrifices foreshadowed the ultimate sacrifice, though, of Christ on the cross. Christ is the fulfillment of the Passover lambs, the sheep, bulls, oxen, doves, and goats that were sacrificed on the temple altar for hundreds and hundreds of years. These sacrifices alone did not atone for sin, but rather, they pointed forward in faith and trust and hope to the promised Messiah, the Christ, Jesus.

Lutherans talk about "Jesus for you" a lot. But do you know what that really means? Jesus is for you. Jesus *died* for you. And not just in an emotional or sentimental sense. To be sure, Jesus did die because He loves and cares for you that much, even unto death! This is what drove Him to the cross. But Jesus also died for you—as in, *in your place*.

You and I deserve death because of our sin, but instead, Jesus died the death we deserve.

We were in the cell waiting for execution, but Jesus took our spot instead—and without us knowing or asking, without anything that would merit it either (see Romans 5:8).

We deserve death. Actually, we deserve more than just death. We deserve *hell*, or eternal death, eternal separation from God. Maybe that's a bit shocking to you. How could a good God say that I deserve death, let alone hell? I didn't sin along with Adam and Eve—I wouldn't be born for thousands of years! That can't be fair, right?

Let's back up a little. What even *is* death and hell anyway? In Genesis, we read that on the first day of creation, God created the heavens and the earth. At some point during the six days of creation, though we don't really know the timeline for this part, God also created angels. Angels are spirit beings, like God, complete without a material body. At some point between the creation of the angels and the fall of man, we are told that "war arose in heaven" (Revelation 12:7) with a number of angels rebelling against God. These fallen angels became demons. They were led by the chief fallen angel, Satan, or the devil. God created him as "an angel of light" (see 2 Corinthians 11:14), which is why we sometimes call him *Lucifer*, which is "light-bearer" in Latin. Satan and the fallen angels that followed him were cast out of heaven. And when Christ returns to judge the world, He will cast them into hell, a place outside the presence of God. How can a place be outside the presence of God when God is present everywhere? I have no idea. That's one of those things that we have to accept on faith rather than trying to make up a logical explanation. But it makes sense, paradoxically: these angels wanted to reject God, and they got their wish; they were cast out from God's presence. But it turns out that's a pretty nasty place, one that Jesus repeatedly describes as full of "weeping and gnashing of teeth" (see Matthew 8:12; Luke 13:28, among others).

Hell, though, was only intended as a place for the rebelling angels because the fall was not in God's original plan (neither was the fall of the angels, though). But when man fell, this caused a problem. As we discussed earlier, sin is a rejection of God. To persist in sin—that is, to refuse the mercy given to us by Jesus, which we also call blaspheming the Holy Spirit—means to persist in rejecting God. If we reject God and His mercy, the only place left for us in the universe is hell.

But what about death? To be sure, God did tell Adam and Eve that if they ate of the fruit of the tree of the knowledge of good and evil, they would surely die (Genesis 2:17). They didn't die immediately, at least not in the way that we think of death. In another, spiritual way, though, they did die: they lost the ability to live in harmony with God, to do good, to be pleasing to God. They became alienated from Him. They became enslaved to sin, enslaved to the undoing of all that is good and God-pleasing in the universe.

But that was just Adam and Eve, right? Well, the Church has taught that, in a way we don't really understand, Adam and Eve didn't act alone in that moment. We *all* fell with them. Sometimes we can be tempted to read the account of the fall, or any other unhappily ending Bible story for that matter, and assume that we'd be better, we'd do the right thing, we wouldn't sin, if it had just been us rather than them. It's very tempting to do this with the fall. But it's also utterly wrong.

In a cosmic, mysterious way, we were there at the fall: we, too, sinned. When our first human parents sinned, we inherited all the same weaknesses and faults Adam and Eve had after the fall. Outside of Christ, we can do no good thing! We may think it unjust for God to assign Adam and Eve's guilt to all of us, their children, but God alone has the right to make the rules that govern His creatures, and we must live by His rules or face His judgment and wrath.

Additionally, we also now carry their "sin nature" in us. All people born of the union of a man and a woman carry this inborn inclination to sin, also called concupiscence, in their very bones and in their very soul. Because Jesus was born of a virgin, He didn't—again, we don't know how, but somehow the union of man and woman passes on the sinful nature to any and all children produced in that way. From the moment of our conception, we are unable to choose God or do good: we are slaves to sin from the very beginning.

And if this all wasn't enough, we also actively sin—each and every one of us, each and every day. In the age of constant media and *social* media consumption, it can be easy to compare ourselves favorably to other people. Chances are you have never committed a heinous and grotesque crime. Chances are you know somebody you look down on because they're always messing up, hurting people, breaking the law, or just being a deadweight on their family or society. And sure, maybe you haven't done anything that would get you arrested and put away for life. But regardless of whether you have or haven't, you have sinned. You have not loved the Lord your God with all your heart, soul, and mind, and you have not loved your neighbor as yourself. You have desperately hurt people, including the people you love.

But we don't want to do these things, or at least we don't want to do *all* of these things. Oftentimes, we do something hurtful or wrong and feel guilt or remorse afterward—and yet often, we fall back into the same patterns of hurt, wrongdoing, and sin. We don't want to yell at our kids (or snap back at our parents), and yet we do. We don't want to gossip about our friends and neighbors, and yet we do. We don't want to shirk responsibility and let down the people who rely on us, and yet we do. Why? Why do we keep repeating this horrible pattern of sin?

As we discussed earlier, the fall affected all of mankind. Adam and Eve do not bear the consequences alone; we are all fallen as a result of their fall into sin. Imparted to us is original sin, which is a complete absence of all that was good and God-pleasing about our identity as human beings made in the image of God. Original sin, however, is not only an absence of the good; it is also an active desire to *undo* what is good and to do what is evil.

God created us with a will. To a certain extent, our will is free; you truly chose for yourself which socks to wear (or whether to wear socks at all) today, whether or not to go to college, get married, buy the house, lease the car, and so on. You are not a robot or a puppet, manipulated by some kind of sadist god for his own entertainment. You are not a mere slave of your physical makeup and the chemicals in your body either, the atheist version of this kind of theology of mankind. You do have a will that is free and able to choose what to do and what not to do in many situations.

But your will is not completely free, and you are not completely independent. We see this at a psychological level: a person's upbringing, family, and life experiences are all limiting factors on what a person is able to do. None of us can *truly* do *anything* we want to. But our lack of independence goes far deeper than just limiting our career choices or life trajectory. The human will is bound, it is not free, with respect to sin and righteousness. Original sin is so ingrained and pervasive in the human heart that we *cannot* choose to do that which is good of our own accord. Instead, we choose *not* to do what is good, or even to do what is sinful and evil. Our concupiscence, our inborn sinful desire, expresses itself actively through our actions.

Maybe you think this a bit harsh. It certainly sounds pretty extreme, and it is rather counter-cultural among many people and groups that believe in our ability to progress toward a better, fairer, more just society through our own striving and actions—sentiments that are present in almost every social and political group and movement regardless of their position on the ideological spectrum. Try telling a person at a dinner party that mankind is unable to choose to do that which is good and improve itself, and you'll be in for a long debate. (Trust me on this one—I'm speaking from experience!)

To a certain extent, we can show this through an honest look at our past and our present. Most depictions of history, especially the history of Europe and America, present the story as an ever-bettering, upward-trending hero's journey, where we continuously strive to reach higher and higher levels of freedom and equality. But if we actually look at the past and the problems around us today, we see that this just isn't true. Every age struggles with sins and vices peculiar to it. We may pride ourselves on how we wouldn't dream of enacting a feudal serf system, enslaving people because of the color of their skin, denying women economic rights, burning people alive for having different religious views, or whatever other historic sins that we ourselves do not struggle with. But our current age has plenty of its own. From the genocide of minority and physically or mentally disabled babies at the hands of abortionists across America, to the slavery that powers the garment industry around the world, to the total disregard for the rights and dignity of the aging and the sick, to the open and violent persecution of Christians around the world, we can be blind to the societal failings of our own day. And these are only problems that will end up in future history textbooks. What about the wrongdoing you have been directly complicit in? What about the people you have slandered, murdered in your heart, lusted after in your thoughts, cheated out of time or goods, betrayed, abandoned, hurt, or failed? What about all those things that you said you would do and did not? All those promises made and broken? All those harsh words spoken? All those dark deeds committed? All those wicked thoughts considered?

This is where we need Scripture to complete the picture.

While we can see that human nature is prone to evil by just looking around us, we need God's Word to reveal the full extent of our sinfulness.

The Bible speaks often about the heart. As modern readers, we may miss the full meaning of this "heart" language. When we talk about the heart today, we either are speaking about the anatomical and medical realities of the engine of the circulatory system pumping blood around our body, or we are talking about our feelings and wishes, like princess movies telling us to "follow your heart" or pop songs entreating us to "listen to your heart." Neither of these is really what the Bible means when it speaks of our heart. The heart was understood symbolically to be the essence of what made a person him- or herself. Your thoughts and wishes and words and actions all come from the heart. It was considered to be the core of a person's being: the truest self, the seat of personality, the steering wheel directing a person's whole life.

Let's bear all of this in mind when we start looking at how the Bible speaks about man's heart. The Bible has a lot to say about our heart—and it isn't good news for us. Before God sent the flood, He "saw that the wickedness of man was great in the earth, and that every intention of the thoughts of his heart was only evil continually" (Genesis 6:5). Psalms and Proverbs especially speak of the wretched state of our hearts: "Everyone utters lies to his neighbor; with flattering lips and a double heart they speak" (Psalm 12:2); "I am feeble and crushed; I groan because of the tumult of my heart" (Psalm 38:8); "[God] knows the secrets of the heart" (Psalm 44:21); "Their heart is unfeeling like fat"

(Psalm 119:70); "Those of crooked heart are an abomination to the LORD" (Proverbs 11:20); "Who can say, 'I have made my heart pure; I am clean from my sin'?" (Proverbs 20:9). Yet we are instructed in the Old Testament and again in the New Testament from Jesus Himself, "You shall love the LORD your God with all your heart and with all your soul and with all your might [mind]" (Deuteronomy 6:5; Matthew 22:37). The Hebrew language has a fondness for repetition and parallelism, which is evident here; in saying that we ought to love God with our entire heart, soul, and might, we underscore that our entire being ought to be one of love and submission to God. Everything we think, say, and do ought to be flowing out of an all-encompassing love of God. And yet, our heart is wicked, an unfeeling stone, unable to even fathom how to truly love God.

Jesus tells us, "Out of the abundance of the heart the mouth speaks" (Matthew 12:34; see also Luke 6:45). When Martin Luther translated this passage, he rendered it a bit more vividly: "What fills up the heart overflows out of the mouth."[2] The Bible tells us that our heart is full of sin as a result of the fall. If our heart is full of sin, then Jesus tells us that everything we say and do will be, too, because the core of our being is turned away from God and pursues instead evil, death, and sin. This is a dire sentence! What can we possibly do to avert certain doom?

We can't do anything. But Jesus can, and He did. Jesus died so that you wouldn't have to.

---

2 English is author's translation of Luther's German Bible.

Jesus Died for Your Sin

Do you wear a cross or crucifix or display one in your house? More than likely, your church has at least one in the sanctuary. Has it ever made you uncomfortable or made someone visiting your home or church uncomfortable? Maybe you've even heard someone compare wearing a cross or crucifix necklace to wearing an electric-chair necklace or a lethal-injection necklace.

Those people actually have a point. If Jesus had been killed using one of those methods, we probably *would* wear necklaces and have church art depicting it. And, yes, crucifixion was a truly horrible way to die. It was slow, painful, and humiliating. People were crucified naked in front of large, mocking crowds. It was an utter abomination, a horrific spectacle, and an absolutely inhumane, disturbing, downright evil event. We can't and shouldn't deny that.

So why do we wear necklaces that depict the death of Jesus—the death of God Himself, the absolute low point of all of history? Because it's the entire point of being Christian. It's the most important thing to happen in the whole universe.

The crucifixion is not an allegory or a fable. It's not a feel-better story, an example to show you how to overcome a really bad day. It's not a metaphor, or a myth, or just another example of an archetype story. (To be sure, we can find "Christ figures" in works of fiction and identify biblical imagery, especially related to the crucifixion, in works of art, but Jesus' death is so much more than a literary trope.) Sometimes, people are tempted to minimize the crucifixion, either by turning it into a metaphor or an object lesson or by trying to avoid it entirely. But we can't. The moment we do, we lose everything.

If we deny or look away from Jesus on the cross, we turn our backs on God and His saving plan for us.

So let's look at the cross head-on.

The cross is all about *substitutionary atonement*. Maybe you're familiar with this term, or maybe not, but it's worth taking time to look closely at what the words that make up this term mean.

Substitutionary means that Jesus takes your place. He's your substitute. He's doing something *for you*, like a proxy or a fill-in. What that means, though, is that the cross was meant for you: it was your punishment, your just deserts, your sentence.

Atonement is often defined as "at-one-ment," to be made whole or unified. It's the payment for sin, the way to right a wrong, reconciliation. At Jesus' death, the sins of the whole world were paid for. All of humanity is made whole again by being united to Christ. Jesus' body and soul were broken in order that your body and soul would be united to His in His saving death and resurrection.

So let's put that all together: Jesus pays the price for *your* sins. He takes *your* debt and pays it all. Maybe you've heard these phrases before—and maybe many times. They can start to lose their meaning after a while. So let's put it this way: you deserved to die on that cross, to be beaten, stripped, and humiliated, tortured and killed, utterly abandoned by God. Your sin—your sinful heart and your sinful thoughts, words, and deeds—merited nothing but death and separation from God, or hell. But Jesus, true God and true man, stepped in and said, "I will take this cup from you." God poured out His wrath against all of humanity—against all the genocides, all the wars, all the murders, all the adulteries, all the sexual immorality, all the idolatry, all the gossip, all the disobedience, all the hatred, all the apathy. From Adam and Eve rejecting God's good will and taking the fruit to the horrors of twentieth-century mass murder, to all of those secret sins you have committed and tried to hide in your heart.

Every single ounce of wrath that God felt for the horrors wrought by His creation, all of it, fell on Jesus. The crucifixion of Jesus was far worse than a Roman torture device and a mocking Jewish crowd: God the Father Himself turned His back on Jesus in order that He would never do the same to you.

Hell became incarnate at the cross, the pain and suffering and unfathomable loneliness and insurmountable distance from the Father's love, so that you would never, ever, *ever* have to feel it. Jesus died for you: He died because you deserved to die, but He died instead because He loves you.

It's the worst trade ever—and the best. Jesus made Himself nothing so that you would have everything—and completely free of charge. Jesus' death is an all-atoning sacrifice—everything is paid for. In Christ's own words, "It is finished" (John 19:30). Jesus has done everything necessary to free us from our sin, from our guilt, from our death, and from our deserved punishment.

Everything! There's nothing left for you to do. Literally, absolutely, nothing.

Theologians have called this "the great exchange." We give Jesus our sin, and He gives us His righteousness. We give Jesus our death, and He gives us His life. We give Jesus our punishment, and He gives us His blessedness.

As St. Paul writes, "For our sake He made Him to be sin who knew no sin, so that in Him we might become the righteousness of God" (2 Corinthians 5:21). In other words, Jesus not only took away but *became*—not metaphorically or symbolically but literally *became*—our sin in order that He could suffer our punishment and give us His righteousness.

This is also what our cornerstone of Lutheran faith—"Justification by grace alone through faith alone"— means. That's another phrase that's worth breaking down, whether or not it's familiar to you.

"Justification" is the process by which we become justified, or made right with and reconciled to God. None of us were right with God because all of us have sinned and fallen short of the glory of God (Romans 3:23). When we are justified, however, the rift between us and God is healed, and the relationship is restored.

"By grace alone" means that we don't do the work of justification ourselves. It is a gift! We are not justified by our own works but rather by the work of Jesus dying on the cross to restore us to the Father. We can't save ourselves, which is why God, out of His infinite mercy, sent His own Son to save us instead.

But how do we receive this gift? "Through faith alone." Faith isn't an action that we do—instead, it is worked within our hearts by the Holy Spirit. "Faith" means belief or trust, and the important thing is faith's object. Everyone has faith in something, and a lot of people have faith in themselves and their own abilities; they think they can justify themselves. Or maybe they think that they have earned salvation, or even deserve God's forgiveness! This isn't faith. Faith is all about Jesus: believing that Jesus' death is enough, trusting that Jesus has saved you. We can't do anything to merit or earn this salvation, but it is possible to reject it. If a person rejects the gift of faith, also called blaspheming the Holy Spirit, unto death, they have rejected the gift of God and the work of Jesus and have chosen to rely on their own works apart from God. They have chosen hell. We will talk more about that in the fourth chapter, but for now, the important thing is that this gift of salvation is free: you are justified by grace through faith. "For by grace you have been saved through faith. And this is not your own doing; it is the gift of God, not a result of works, so that no one may boast" (Ephesians 2:8–9).

Jesus died for your sin. The eternal Son, the very Word of God, who made the heavens and the earth, chose to die a painful, humiliating death. And He did it all for you. It's not a metaphor. It's not a symbol. It's not a myth or a story or a fable. Jesus died. His holy heart stopped beating and His sinless mouth ceased to breathe. The very Author of life let the life ebb out of His body so that you would not die in your sin, alone and separated from God. Jesus died so that you would live, and live sinlessly, deathlessly, eternally.

Jesus Rose from the Dead

But this isn't the end. Jesus didn't just die—He also rose from the dead. And that is a very, very big deal.

The Bible doesn't give us many instances of people being raised from the dead. We read of a few in the Old Testament, like the widow of Zarephath's son, who Elijah raised from the dead in 1 Kings 17:17–24. In the New Testament, during the earthly ministry of Christ, the Gospels record Jesus raising three people from the dead: the daughter of Jairus, the synagogue ruler (Mark 5:21–24, 35–43), the son of the widow of Nain (Luke 7:11–17), and Lazarus (John 11:1–44). After Christ's ascension, the apostles also raised some people from the dead, such as the youth Eutychus, who fell asleep on a window sill, fell to his death, and was subsequently raised from the dead by the apostle Paul (Acts 20:7–12).

Sometimes the awe of one of these resurrection accounts can be lost on us. Medicine has advanced so much since Bible times that it's not uncommon to hear of—or even know someone who has personally experienced—near-death experiences, or of someone's heart stopping or brain activity shutting down and then coming back. In some heart surgeries, for example, a surgeon might induce hypothermialike conditions, rendering the person's body indistinguishable from a lifeless corpse, conduct the life-saving surgery, and then restore warmth and life to the body.[3] These "return from the dead" stories are now relatively commonplace, at least enough that they are sometimes used by non-Christians to refute our claims that resurrection is a big deal. It's important to note, however, that this isn't the kind of

3 Kevin Fong, "Surgeons Use Cold to Suspend Life," September 27, 2010, https://www.bbc.com/news/health-11389464.

death we are talking about when dealing with a resurrection in the Bible. These modern-day examples are not really death from a theological point of view. Sure, there is a (temporary) cessation of biological processes necessary to life, and normally, this clinical death is indistinguishable from what we understand death to be from a theological standpoint, with the above exceptions. But let's look closer at the theological implications of death.

If you recall, "The wages of sin is death" (Romans 6:23). We have already established the seriousness of sin in this chapter—so it wouldn't make sense that the wages of sin, the just punishment for total rejection of and attempted coup against the Creator of the universe, would be a flatlining electrocardiogram that reverses itself. Instead, the Church has understood death to be the permanent separation of the soul from the body (with exceptions for divine intervention through miracles like those mentioned above and for the eventual return of Christ to raise all the dead—more on that in chapter four).

The widow of Nain's son wasn't just in an artificially induced cold state, and Lazarus wasn't just declared brain dead. These people were *dead*, clinically and theologically. Lazarus had been in the grave so long—four days!—that Martha and Mary were concerned about the smell in the tomb, a gross detail that nevertheless underscores the seriousness of this miracle. Jesus didn't just warm up Lazarus's body or restore his normal brain function. He reunited Lazarus's body and soul.[4] He undid the early stages of decomposition. Jesus did here what God did through

4 It is worth mentioning here that we receive no indication from the text of what that interim period was like for Lazarus, though we have clearer indications elsewhere in Scripture of the nature of the intermediate state of the soul after death and awaiting resurrection, namely, heaven. We will get to that in greater detail in chapter four.

Ezekiel when the prophet spoke over the dry bones and "the bones came together . . . and flesh had come upon them, and skin had covered them," and the Lord breathed life—their very souls—back into them (Ezekiel 37:1–10).

These raisings of dead people in the Bible are examples of God showcasing His power and mercy to mankind, either directly in the person of Jesus Christ or through a prophet or apostle like Elijah or Paul. God uses these as a way to prove these individuals are who they claim to be, which is why it sometimes caused a ruckus when Christ raised dead people—He was providing evidence that He was who He said He was, namely, the Son of God incarnate.

These raisings of the dead are different from Jesus Christ's resurrection, however. No prophet raised Him—the triune God did, Father, Son, and Holy Spirit. Jesus predicted His resurrection, saying, "Destroy this temple, and in three days I will raise it up" (John 2:19). The Father and Holy Spirit were active too: "God the Father, who raised [Jesus Christ] from the dead" (Galatians 1:1), and "For Christ also suffered once for sins, the righteous for the unrighteous, that He might bring us to God, being put to death in the flesh but made alive in the spirit" (1 Peter 3:18).

If Jesus died and that were the end of the story, none of this would matter. If Jesus died and that were the end of the story, you shouldn't be a Christian. Maybe that sounds off, possibly even blasphemous to you. But consider what St. Paul himself writes in his first epistle to the Church at Corinth:

> **Now if Christ is proclaimed as raised from the dead, how can some of you say that there is no**

resurrection of the dead? But if there is no resurrection of the dead, then not even Christ has been raised. And if Christ has not been raised, then our preaching is in vain and your faith is in vain. We are even found to be misrepresenting God, because we testified about God that He raised Christ, whom He did not raise if it is true that the dead are not raised. For if the dead are not raised, not even Christ has been raised. And if Christ has not been raised, your faith is futile and you are still in your sins. Then those also who have fallen asleep in Christ have perished. If in Christ we have hope in this life only, we are of all people most to be pitied. (1 Corinthians 15:12-19)

If Jesus had died but hadn't risen from the dead, He wouldn't have been who He claimed to be. He promised to come back from the dead. If He'd broken that promise, He couldn't have been God. Let's go back to the passage in John where Jesus promises to die and rise again. Here's that same verse in a bit more context:

The Passover of the Jews was at hand, and Jesus went up to Jerusalem. In the temple He found those who were selling oxen and sheep and

> pigeons, and the money-changers sitting there. And making a whip of cords, He drove them all out of the temple, with the sheep and oxen. And He poured out the coins of the money-changers and overturned their tables. And He told those who sold the pigeons, "Take these things away; do not make My Father's house a house of trade." His disciples remembered that it was written, "Zeal for Your house will consume Me."
>
> So the Jews said to Him, "What sign do You show us for doing these things?" Jesus answered them, "Destroy this temple, and in three days I will raise it up." The Jews then said, "It has taken forty-six years to build this temple, and will You raise it up in three days?" But He was speaking about the temple of His body. When therefore He was raised from the dead, His disciples remembered that He had said this, and they believed the Scripture and the word that Jesus had spoken. (John 2:13–22)

So Jesus goes into the temple and causes a ruckus by driving out the money-changers. This is actually a fulfillment of multiple Old Testament prophecies about the coming Messiah, including Psalm 69:9 (quoted in the text, "Zeal for Your house will consume

Me") and Zechariah 14:21 ("And there shall no longer be a trader in the house of the LORD of hosts on that day"). Nevertheless, they demand a sign from Jesus to prove that He has the authority to do this. They misunderstand Jesus' promise, thinking that He means the actual temple in Jerusalem, around which they are gathered. But after Jesus' death and third-day resurrection, the disciples remembered this moment and understood it.

They understood the same thing you and I do now: that Jesus' resurrection was a miracle of miracles, a great sign to Jew and Gentile alike that Jesus is true God and our true Savior.

All hope seemed to be lost—God Himself *died*! And yet, from this, the low point of all time, sprang forth the best thing that has ever happened. He—Jesus Christ, God in the flesh—came back from the dead.

What does all of this mean? The Christian faith centers around Christ—His death and His resurrection. These are historical, verifiable events, as we discussed in chapter one. But they are so much more than historical facts or dates on a timeline. They are powerful mysteries—things we can't fully understand and never will.

Imagine the surprise of the women when they met the angel at the empty tomb. Imagine the shock the disciples felt when they saw Jesus for the first time after His resurrection. Jesus overcame death itself, vanquishing the terror of all creation, and He did it so that you would likewise know life after death. For even though you die, God will raise you from the dead, just like He raised Christ, because death, sin, and the devil himself have been vanquished on your behalf. Rejoice! For Christ's resurrection is your resurrection too.

Jesus Died and Rose for You

How does Jesus' death and resurrection help us understand our identity? For starters, Jesus' death shows us the severity of our sinfulness. It can be tempting to rationalize our ill tempers, our apathetic ears, our gossiping lips, our hate-harboring hearts. It's easy to blame other people, our upbringing, the state of the world today, how much sleep we got last night, or any number of unfortunate circumstances that might befall us. Or maybe we don't realize it at all—maybe we don't recognize that those biting jokes and less-than-honest practices at work and mocking interior monologue in our head are ways of rejecting God and His plan for our lives.

We dishonor God and harm our neighbor in a thousand tiny ways every single day by our thoughts, words, and deeds. Considering this overwhelming weight of our sin—how inescapable it can feel to resist falling again and again into hurt and rebellion—can be nothing short of crushing.

This is why Jesus had to die. The weight of our sin—all of it collectively as well as each of our sins as individuals—demanded a sacrifice, one that we could never hope to make on our own. So Jesus stepped into our position and bore the full wrath of the all-just and sinless God against His rebellious and hate-filled creation. Whenever we feel tempted to push our sins under the rug, to argue away our faithless deeds and loveless words, we should return to Christ's cross, in somber remembrance of the true cost of our wrongdoing.

But the cross and empty tomb of Christ tell us something else. The cross is the ultimate expression of God's love for us. Jesus says, "Greater love has no one than this, that someone lay down his life for his friends" (John 15:13). This is exactly what Jesus does for all of us—for you, dear reader. Jesus loves you enough to die for you. Not because of anything you did—you didn't deserve or earn God's love, a love that is all gift in spite of what you deserve because of your sin. And the cross doesn't just symbolize this love metaphorically. No, the cross *creates*. Jesus' death and resurrection creates a new reality, one where your sins have been atoned for and you are set free from sin and all its effects. Sure, for now, you still linger in this vale of tears, where you struggle against your inborn inclination to sin and face the consequences of sickness, infirmity, and death. But it will not be forever. In fact, you are already dwelling in the holy presence of God, made perfect through Christ, which we'll explain in the next chapter.

After his fall into adultery with Bathsheba, King David penned a penitential psalm that has remained in constant use throughout the history of the Church. You probably know at least part of it if you have ever attended a Lutheran worship service:

Create in me a clean heart, O God,
and renew a right spirit within me.
Cast me not away from Your presence,
and take not Your Holy Spirit from me.

Restore to me the joy of Your salvation,
and uphold me with a willing spirit.
(Psalm 51:10–12)

That heart of ours, the seat of our whole being that has been wrecked by sin? It is now transformed. It is now turned back toward God, enlivened to do good works, full of the peace and joy that passes all understanding that God alone can provide.

We may not always feel like this transformation can be true, but it remains true nevertheless. The hardest battle and greatest victory of all time has already been won: the battle between God and Satan for your very soul. Spoiler alert: God has already won. Jesus crushed sin, death, and the devil into oblivion with His nail-pierced feet, and just like He threw open His own tomb on that first Easter, He has thrown open the door of your heart and established there His throne, which nothing can ever overcome.

What did Jesus do? A lot of things, most of which would be easier for us to think about. Jesus' death is hard for us to face. Death itself is always painful, but the death of God Himself? Jesus Christ, the only-begotten Son of God, Prince of Peace and merciful Lord, who came as an innocent, helpless babe, suffered all the pain and weakness we feel throughout our lives only to be unjustly arrested, indicted, and tortured to death for preaching the Good News that He—God Himself—came to save us from our sin? At times, thinking about His death can be more than our hearts can bear.

But the story doesn't end there. Jesus came back from the dead. Think back to Jesus raising Lazarus and to Ezekiel in the valley of dry bones. I know both stories can be a little gross, especially if you're like me and are rather squeamish, but they are very important to understanding what Jesus has done for you and me. You were dead in sin, as dead as the valley of dry bones. You were unable to please God or love neighbor. But God did not abandon you to that fate. Instead, Jesus destroyed death by dying and then rising so that you, too, would be resurrected, first your heart but eventually your body, too, when Jesus comes to establish His kingdom in the remade heaven and earth. What Ezekiel did on a small scale to foreshadow the Messiah, Jesus will do to all creation—to *you*—and will undo sin and death in their entirety.

What did Jesus do? Jesus died for you to save you. Jesus took away your sin, guilt, and punishment, and He gives you His righteousness, sinlessness, and blessedness. Thanks be to God!

CHAPTER TWO STUDY QUESTIONS

1. Read Isaiah 53, a prophecy about the death and saving work of Jesus Christ. Meditate on it individually or as a group. What picture does the prophet Isaiah paint of Christ?

2. Read the following "I am" statements from Jesus: "I am the Good Shepherd" (John 10:11–18); "I and the Father are one" (John 10:30); "Before Abraham was, I am" (John 8:58). Why are these passages significant? Why did Jesus' audience become so angry with Him over these statements?

3. How does the Bible define evil, sin, and death? How are the three related?

4. In what way do we have free will? In what way do we not have free will?

5. What does the Bible have to say about our heart? Why is that important? (Look at pp. 70–71 for a list of relevant Bible passages.)

6. What does substitutionary atonement mean? Why is it important?

7. Read 1 Corinthians 15:12–19. On what event is our faith based?

8. **What makes Jesus' resurrection similar to and different from other raisings of the dead in the Bible, such as that of the widow of Zarephath's son or Lazarus?**

9. **What do Jesus' death and resurrection tell us about our identity?**

10. **What did Jesus do? Why is this important?**

CHAPTER THREE

WHERE IS JESUS NOW?

Sometimes, when we read the Bible, it can be tempting to be jealous of the disciples. They saw, heard, touched, and spoke with Jesus, after all! If we just had that experience, we might think to ourselves, then we wouldn't struggle with doubt so much. If Jesus weren't so far away, if He were here, then our faith would finally be as strong as we wish it were.

But what if Jesus *is* here with us?

Despite growing up Christian, it wasn't until I became Lutheran that I started understanding that Jesus hadn't abandoned humanity—abandoned *me*—at His ascension. The Lutheran Church has always taught the historic Christian view that Jesus is present in real ways through specific means, a teaching that is found in the Bible and that provides a great deal of comfort and hope to believers. But, in our world of cold rationalism and skeptical doubt, even other Christians sometimes disagree with us on this teaching. It's important, therefore, to read and meditate on the words of Scripture carefully and in great humility so that we can recognize and cherish Jesus' presence among us to forgive and sanctify us.

Jesus Ascended into Heaven

The final chapter of the Book of Luke and the first chapter of the Book of Acts tell us that forty days after the resurrection, Jesus ascended into heaven. Here's what the Bible has to say about it. In Luke's Gospel, the evangelist writes:

And [Jesus] led them out as far as Bethany, and lifting up His hands He blessed them. While

He blessed them, He parted from them and was carried up into heaven.

And they worshiped Him and returned to Jerusalem with great joy, and were continually in the temple blessing God. (Luke 24:50–53)

And then, in Acts, Luke also writes:

So when they had come together, they asked [Jesus], "Lord, will You at this time restore the kingdom to Israel?" He said to them, "It is not for you to know the times or seasons that the Father has fixed by His own authority. But you will receive power when the Holy Spirit has come upon you, and you will be My witnesses in Jerusalem and in all Judea and Samaria, and to the end of the earth." And when He had said these things, as they were looking on, He was lifted up, and a cloud took Him out of their sight. And while they were gazing into heaven as He went, behold, two men stood by them in white robes, and said, "Men of Galilee, why do you stand looking into heaven? This Jesus, who was taken up from you

into heaven, will come in the same way as you saw Him go into heaven." (Acts 1:6–11)

It may seem like Jesus' ministry ends rather abruptly, even anticlimactically, after His resurrection. It may even seem like His ascension contradicts Jesus' last words in the Gospel of Matthew: "And behold, I am with you always, to the end of the age" (Matthew 28:20). If Jesus has gone up into heaven, then how can He be with us always?

Lutherans have a very unique and helpful way of making sense of this apparent paradox. Like we talked about in the first two chapters, Jesus is fully God and fully man, but He did not always make full use of His divinity. This was called His "humiliation," because He humbled Himself, even to the point of death on a cross (see Philippians 2:8). But, beginning with the resurrection, Jesus starts doing something new: He begins what is called His "exaltation," where He makes full use of His divinity (while never giving up His humanity—or, as we see when Jesus lets Thomas place his hand in His pierced side, the wounds inflicted upon Him during the crucifixion, the pinnacle of His humiliation).

After hiding His divinity in order to be our substitute, Jesus now exerts it to prove that He is the Lord of Life, who has conquered death itself.

We see this in some of the miracles performed after the resurrection, like when Jesus miraculously appears in the locked upper room. No mere man could walk through a wall! But He is still a man—He eats with His disciples and walks with the men on the road to Emmaus (Luke 24:13–49).

But why the ascension? If we go a couple chapters forward in the Book of Acts, we start to get an answer. In Acts 3, Peter is speaking to a crowd of Jewish men at a place outside of the temple in Jerusalem called Solomon's Portico. Peter preaches to them, rebuking them for rejecting Jesus and exhorting them to repent and confess Jesus as the Messiah. As part of this sermon, Peter describes the ascension and the second coming (more on that in the next chapter): "Repent therefore, and turn back, that your sins may be blotted out, that times of refreshing may come from the presence of the Lord, and that He may send the Christ appointed for you, Jesus, whom heaven must receive until the time for restoring all the things about which God spoke by the mouth of His holy prophets long ago" (Acts 3:19–21).

This sentence is a mouthful, so let's work through it slowly. First, Peter tells the crowd to repent of rejecting and crucifying Jesus (see Acts 3:13–15), in order to receive forgiveness for their sins and refreshment, or new life. Jesus was the prophesied Messiah, which His ascension proves, and He will return at the end of the world to restore the universe.

When Martin Luther translated this passage in his German Bible, he made an interesting choice. Whereas the English Standard Version translates Acts 3:21 as "[Jesus], whom heaven must receive," Martin Luther translated it as something like, "Jesus, who enters heaven," or even, "Jesus, who conquers heaven."[5]

Maybe these two translations don't seem that different, but it's actually very important to how Lutherans understand the ascension. During the Reformation, other Protestant groups followed in

5 English is author's translation of Luther's German Bible.

the wake of Luther, leaving the Catholic Church to enact reform and establish their own churches. Many of these theologians and groups went further than Luther, changing and introducing more things than Luther and his followers were comfortable with. For example, the followers of John Calvin, who became what is now known as the Presbyterian or Reformed Church, like Luther, rejected the Roman Catholic teachings on transubstantiation, which says that the "substances" of the bread and wine in Holy Communion are "transformed" completely; they cease to be bread and wine—they only *look* like bread and wine—and are only the body and blood of Jesus.

John Calvin and his followers, like the Lutherans, rejected this understanding of the Sacrament because it can't be found in the Bible; the idea of "substances" and "appearances" (also called "accidents") comes from the Greek philosopher Aristotle, not the Scriptures. However, John Calvin went further than Luther. Whereas Luther said that the Lord's Supper was *both* the body *and* bread and the blood *and* wine, Calvin taught that the bread and the wine were only *spiritually* Jesus' body and blood; Jesus didn't come down to believers in the Lord's Supper, but rather believers spiritually ascended to heaven to commune with Jesus.

Calvin and his followers argued this in part because of their understanding of the ascension. Jesus was in heaven, they said, and can't be in two places at once in His body, because that's not how human bodies work. Therefore, it would seem to make more sense that the believer would spiritually ascend to Jesus, who is in heaven until the second coming.

Luther and his followers, especially a German theologian named Martin Chemnitz (sometimes called the "Second Martin" for his important role in keeping the Lutheran Church together in the hectic decades following Luther's death), took another view, though. Unlike Calvin, the Lutherans viewed Christ's ascension as a proof of His triumph over sin, death, and the devil. He entered heaven, not as a physically bound location where He would physically remain, in a sense trapped until His second coming but rather as a declaration of victory, a culmination of His glorification. Jesus, His suffering completed and our debt to the Father rectified, now makes full use of His divinity—meaning that, yes, against the laws of nature, He can be present in multiple locations at once, in heaven and in the fonts and on the altars of churches across the world.

The ascension wasn't Jesus being "sent to His room" to wait for the end of the world. The ascension was how Jesus accomplished His promise to "be with you always": fully glorified, He now is with us always in His Word and in the Sacraments.

Jesus Is Present in His Word

What do we mean by "the Word"? For starters, Jesus Himself *is* the Word, the eternal, creative Word, through which the whole universe was made. This Word became flesh, St. John tells us, and dwelt among us, and this Word is Jesus (John 1:14). But this divine Word isn't like our words. Most of the time, our words are descriptive: we talk about the world around us as it already is. Sometimes our words are hopeful or hypothetical, and sometimes they ask other people to do things. In a few situations, our words can create promises, or oaths, like at a wedding or a confirmation. We swear faithfulness to our confession of faith or to our spouse, which are important words of a very different nature than most of our humdrum everyday words. But even then, we can go back—and we do go back—on these words. Marriages are dissolved, faith is lost, and even the everyday doubt, restlessness, apathy, and busyness weakens the lofty heights that our oath-words aspire to. No man, then, can create by his words. But God can.

Before the beginning of time and space, God spoke. And what did He say? "Let there be light" (Genesis 1:3). This wasn't a description of how the universe already was—light *literally did not exist* until that moment, which is a bit difficult to imagine. This wasn't a request, either, nor a man-made promise or oath that could be broken or weakened.

This divine Word is Jesus. The Word that created the universe is the Word made flesh who dwells among us. And as a result, Jesus continues to be present—literally present—whenever this Word, His Word, is proclaimed.

It's also worth mentioning that the Holy Spirit is also present whenever the Word of God is proclaimed. We tend to make one of two errors with regard to the Holy Spirit. We often gloss over Him, forgetting that He is an active member of the Trinity or speaking in totally incorrect ways about Him. A lot of people think that the Holy Spirit is an impersonal force, this sort of power that can be channeled or that inspires thoughts and feelings. The Holy Spirit does empower us to do good works and to think, speak, and act in God-pleasing ways, but the Holy Spirit is *not* a force. He is a divine person, just like the Father and the Son are. The Holy Spirit, in other words, isn't an "it" but is instead a "He."

Other times, the Holy Spirit is wrongfully exalted above the other two persons of the Trinity. Sometimes, people end up making the Holy Spirit more important than Jesus, though they probably don't mean to. When certain teachers and church bodies emphasize the importance of exhibiting certain spiritual abilities or gifts, sometimes also called "marks of the Holy Spirit," they turn people's eyes away from Jesus and onto the Holy Spirit. Some church bodies, for example, make a big deal out of the ability to speak in tongues, a spiritual gift that is seen in the Book of Acts and that Paul discusses in a few brief passages. The Holy Spirit does truly work in the hearts of believers throughout time, usually by working in us good works for our neighbor or by driving us to worship, read the Bible, pray, and spend time in devotion. Sometimes, the Holy Spirit also brings miraculous gifts, like the gift of tongues at Pentecost, though these sorts of experiences are not promised to Christians as a whole, nor should they be used as a yard stick of true or better faith. (In fact, seeking after these gifts, usually to the exclusion of the actual gifts of the Holy Spirit and the places where Jesus has promised to be—more on that in a minute—are often detrimental to faith!) This way of thinking about the Holy Spirit ultimately distracts and even detracts from Jesus because it results in thinking more about our abilities and experiences than about the gift of God's mercy given to us through His Son.

The Holy Spirit is significant, then, but He is not greater than the Father and the Son. Instead,

the best way to understand the person, work, and role of the Holy Spirit is by understanding what He loves to do: the Holy Spirit loves pointing you to Jesus. Jesus sent the Holy Spirit after He ascended into heaven in order that we would not be alone.

The Holy Spirit constantly reminds us of Jesus, shows us our sin and Christ's atoning work, tells us that we are forgiven and therefore ought to forgive one another. The Holy Spirit does not want to talk about Himself: He wants to talk about Jesus, which is what we'll get back to doing now.

Wherever the Word is, Jesus is there—really, truly there—for you. And where is the Word? The most obvious answer is the Bible, the written Word of God, passed down from Old Testament times to New Testament times to today. The Bible isn't just an instruction manual, or a history, or a collection of ancient wisdom and poetical texts. The Bible tells us who God is, but God also dwells in His Word.

The Bible is a paradox. Maybe you have spoken with an unbelieving friend or family member about the Bible or even tried to get him or her to read it. I hope you were successful, but most of the time, these attempts are frustrating and fruitless. Why? Well, the Bible is a closed book to nonbelievers. Consider how Jesus Himself spoke to the Pharisees and others who rejected Him throughout the Gospels. Jesus often spoke in parables, commanded others to keep secrets about His teachings or healings, and in some places outright disappears! Theologians even talk about a theme, found especially in the Gospel of Mark, called the "Messianic secret," where Jesus seems to hide His true identity as God and man, the Messiah come to save all humanity, from those who reject Him. After all, Jesus could have been transfigured in front of the Pharisees, opened heaven to the Sadducees, or shown Himself after the resurrection to the temple high priest—but He didn't! This has also confused me, but it helps us understand a little about the Bible, in a roundabout way.

The Bible is a closed book to sinners who are unwilling to recognize their sin and humble themselves before God. There is a mystery here that we will never fully understand: the mystery of election.

Why are some people saved and not others? Why does Jesus reveal Himself to some people in the Bible, while hiding His identity from other people? How come some people read the Bible and turn to Christ, while others read it and turn to ridicule Him? Why does that friend, family member, coworker, or neighbor refuse to come to church when other people you know are becoming Christian from books they read, a video they watched online, or conversations with someone they know? This is the mystery of election. Why does God elect, or choose, to save some people while other people turn from Him in disbelief? The answer is short, simple, and wildly unfulfilling: we don't really know.

Some churches try to resolve this issue by saying the choice lies in each of us. God doesn't force anyone to reject Him, those who do have chosen to do so. And therefore believing in Jesus is our choice also. They teach you must choose to follow Jesus, to let God into your heart, to be forgiven. You choose God, and you choose salvation. But as we talked about in the last chapter, this doesn't really match up with what the Bible says about our abilities and identity after the fall. Because of original sin, we are spiritually dead. We can't choose to be saved because we are enslaved to sin.

When Jesus calls out, "Lazarus, come out," Lazarus doesn't lay there thinking, "Jesus is calling, I better come alive again and go out to Him." Jesus says, "Lazarus, come out" and the power of His divine word makes what He says come to pass—He restores life to Lazarus and the ability to come walking out of his tomb.

With each person Jesus raised from the dead, there was no action on their part because they couldn't contribute anything—remember, they were *dead*! We are like those people, utterly reliant on the life-giving Word of God, unable to choose Him or salvation.

Some people fall into the opposite error, however. Rather than believing we have free will to choose God, some people teach that God predestines some to heaven *and* some to hell, a teaching called double predestination. *Predestination* means that God chose the eternal destination of the soul ahead of time. This doctrine, however, can result in some strange teachings. It can turn people into little more than robots, for one thing—a puppet on a string controlled by a tyrannical God. Additionally, though, it can actually produce a lot of self-doubt and worry about whether or not a person is saved. Some people go so far as to say that God may choose to condemn people who, by all counts, seem to be Christians. Or they encourage people to determine whether or not they are saved by how good their works are. Real saved Christians, they might teach, will know they are saved because they don't sin or because they do lots of good things for other people.

To be sure, it is a good thing to try not to sin and to attempt to do what is right and helpful for one's neighbor. And, additionally, as Lutherans, we teach predestination—though only *single* predestination, which is an important distinction. God truly did, before the foundations of the world, know your heart, and He decided to save you from eternity. It wasn't on you, it wasn't your choice, it wasn't because of anything you did. God, in His infinite mercy, chose you, specifically *you*, to be saved. This should come as a comfort to you!

God does not, however, predestine people to hell. There is divine foreknowledge and omniscience, which just means that God already knows who is going to hell. But it is not the will of God to condemn any person. People go to hell because they reject God—because they desire to be outside of His presence.

Hell is not the cartoon caricature full of rock stars, blue comedians, motorcyclists, and whatever other sarcastic, mid-twentieth-century comic-strip stereotypes have invaded our public psyche. Hell is also not a medieval torture chamber, with demons having fun performing unspeakable things on people. Hell, simply put, is the absence of God, and this is actually much worse. Remember, as we discussed earlier, God Himself is love. All things lovely and good in the universe are reflections of these attributes of God; they originate from God and without Him could not exist. Hence the "weeping and gnashing of teeth" that Jesus so frequently invokes when speaking about hell: God is so utterly absent from hell, in a way that we can't even imagine (and ought not dwell upon). It isn't a place of devious fun or debauchery. It is utter darkness, utter loneliness, utter abandonment; it is what Jesus experienced on the cross so that you wouldn't have to.

But if a person chooses to reject Jesus' sacrifice for them, if they choose to bear their own sin on their head, if they deny God and wish to live as if He does not exist, then God will give them over to their sinful desires; in other words, be careful what you wish for because you might just get it. But it isn't because God has chosen to send someone to hell; that person has chosen to send themselves.

This might seem like a contradiction or a paradox to you. That's because it is. How can God choose to save some people without also choosing to condemn other people? How can God send some people to heaven but people send themselves to hell? It doesn't make sense to our human logic—because our logic is broken by sin. But even if our logic were perfect, we likely still wouldn't get it.

Even before the fall, the human mind was limited and always has been and always will be. We are not supposed to understand the hidden ways of God. This is one of those hidden things.

Our only response is to admit our limitations and say that we can't fully explain it. Instead, we trust in God's Word and His promise that Jesus' sacrifice was sufficient for each and every person because Jesus carried the sins of the entire world to the cross and satisfied God's wrath fully for all of them. Wherever God's Word is, Jesus is, proclaiming the forgiveness of sins won for all by His work on the cross.

Even when we can't see it, God's Word is active wherever it is proclaimed. Preaching, hymns, and the liturgy also proclaim the Word of God, either actually repeating the words of Scripture or sharing and proclaiming the message of the Gospel, the Good News that Jesus has saved us from our sins.

This is why it's so important to be in worship. All of the elements of the worship service proclaim the Word of God. And where that Word is proclaimed, Jesus is with us—not metaphorically but actually, and the Holy Spirit along with Him to point us back to our salvation.

The Word is proclaimed in an especially important place in the Lutheran worship service. At the beginning of the Divine Service, the whole congregation participates in a corporate (or group) confession of our sins, confessing that we have sinned against God and against our neighbor in thought, word, and deed, by what we have done and by what we have left undone. The pastor then turns around (he had been facing in the same direction as the congregation because he is also confessing his sins) and says, "As a called and ordained servant of Christ, and by His authority, I therefore forgive you all your sins in the name of the Father and of the Son and of the Holy Spirit. Amen" (*LSB*, p. 151).

If you have been a lifelong Lutheran or a Lutheran for many years, maybe this part of the service becomes routine to you. (After all, it's basically the first thing we do, so many of us are still a bit groggy and waiting for our morning coffee to kick in.) If you aren't Lutheran, or recently became Lutheran, this part can be absolutely bizarre. How is this man forgiving my sins? Can't only God forgive sins? Isn't this what Roman Catholics teach?

Let's go back to what the Bible has to say about confession and absolution.

Jesus told His disciples that "whatever you bind on earth shall be bound in heaven, and whatever you loose on earth shall be loosed in heaven" (Matthew 18:18). This promise from Jesus is a promise to your pastor, and through him, a promise to you.

From the time of the Old Testament, God has set apart a group of people to do church work. It's not that these people—called priests in the Old Testament and pastors (though sometimes translated "bishops" or "overseers") in the New Testament—were any better than the rest of the people. Far from it! Rather, this separate group was created to maintain order and prevent chaos. A church where everybody was his own pastor would be a messy ball of confusion, and our God loves order, harmony, and unity, not confusion. So He instituted the priesthood, which foreshadowed Jesus, our High Priest, who is Himself the ultimate sacrifice. The priests of the Old Testament pointed forward to Jesus, and the pastors or undershepherds of the New Testament Church, of which we are a part, point backward to Jesus, the Good Shepherd.

Jesus does not want you to be alone, untethered, confused, wandering without His Word and comfort. Yes, He has given us the Bible, a true and holy gift from God. But we are frail, fallen human beings; we are prone to anxiety, worry, and lack of confidence. Not only that but, intrinsic to what it means to be human, we crave interpersonal interaction. We want to see, hear, and speak to people face-to-face. Think about friends or family members you have who live far away from you. It's wonderful to text or email them, but isn't it so much better to talk to them on the phone? Or to have a video call with them? But, really, isn't the best thing when you have an opportunity to speak with them, shake their hand or hug them, listen, smile, cry, and laugh with them, physically dwell with them? Of course it is!

Jesus wants to be with you in this way too.

The ascension was not the end of this kind of contact with Christ; it was just the beginning! Now, Jesus dwells with us through His Word, including the Word He speaks to you through your pastor.

Pastors aren't there just to remind us of Jesus. They are also entrusted with His Word in His stead. Your pastor is like a proxy for Jesus; your pastor speaks on behalf of Jesus, binding and loosing in accordance with Jesus' will.

But what is your pastor binding or loosing? Sins.

When we participate in corporate confession and absolution, the pastor *does* forgive us our sins, but not by his own power or will or ability. He does it all because of and by the promise of Jesus to act through him.

What's the point of this? Doesn't the Bible tell us that our sins are forgiven? It sure does, so rejoice! But our God is a merciful God, who loves to give and give and give of His never-ending loving kindness. And so, because He knows that we are frail and prone to wander, and because He knows that we are both spiritual and physical beings who need both spiritual and physical reassurance, God also sends His mercy to us through the vocal cords of the man in the alb and clerical standing in the front of your sanctuary every Sunday.

If you've ever been to private confession and absolution, the intimate and immediate love of Christ is even more apparent. Private confession and absolution can seem unusual, unnecessary, or just downright intimidating. And while there is no *law* requiring private confession and absolution, it exists as pure gift for you. When you sit in the pastor's office or kneel before the altar and confess those sins that are bothering you—whether that's some huge, maybe even criminal, act or those piddly, petty sins that you fall into day after day, those boring sins that gnaw at your heart but you can't seem to shake—your pastor can speak your very own name and provide the sweet, comforting balm of Jesus' forgiveness to you personally. You can get as close to speaking to Jesus face-to-face as you can experience on this side of paradise in private confession because your pastor is the person that Jesus has chosen to be His emissary, His representative on earth to you, specifically.

Think of it this way: if Jesus showed up at your church on Sunday and said He'd be keeping office hours on Monday to tell people individually, personally, that He died for and forgave them, do you think you'd show up? What if the angel Gabriel had an office in your church and, at any time, you could pop in to talk about your problems, tell him what was bothering you, and ask him to remind you that Jesus loves you and forgives you—would you make an appointment? My guess is yes. I know I would! You have the same opportunity with your pastor. He's sort of like an angel—*angelos* means "messenger," and he's definitely one of those!

And Jesus has put him in your church to give you a real-time, in-person, face-to-face, physical and spiritual representative of the Most High God, someone who, as our hymnal says, "in the stead and by the command of my Lord Jesus Christ" (*LSB*, p. 185) can proclaim to you, personally, that Jesus died for your sins, especially those ones that needle you the most. What a joyous gift! What a loving God!

So, whether corporate or individual, confession and absolution needn't cause you any confusion or anxiety. The absolution that your pastor offers you is not his absolution; it's Jesus' absolution, won on the cross for you. And since we can't go back to the cross, Jesus sends your pastor to bring the cross to you.

Jesus Is Present in His Sacraments

In addition to confession, Jesus also comes to us bodily through Baptism and the Lord's Supper. We call these rites of the church *sacraments*, a word that derives from the Latin translation of the Greek word *mysterion*, which is also the root of our word *mystery*. Why are these things mysteries? Because the Son of God Himself deigns to dwell among us through these means. That is pretty mysterious!

The Lutheran Church has defined a sacrament as any outward sign to which Jesus attaches Himself and the promise of His forgiveness, signs that He Himself promised during His ministry. The Catholic Church, for example, considers marriage, last rites, confirmation, and ordination also to be sacraments, but we do not because Jesus neither instituted nor promised forgiveness of sin and His presence through those rites. (They are all good things to do, though, which is why we still do all of them, though we sometimes call them different things, like "ordination" instead of "holy orders" and "commendation of the dying" instead of "last rites.")

The Sacraments are absolutely vital to what it means to be Lutheran. They are also one of the most confusing things about the Lutheran faith, both to outsiders, new converts, and even lifelong Lutherans. Thankfully, there are many books written by pastors and theologians about the Sacraments, which continue to help us understand them today.

The Lutheran Church's teachings on the Sacraments make us different from most of the other Christian denominations, especially many of those that are popular in certain parts of America, whether that's Catholics in the Midwest, Baptists in the South, or nondenominational mega churches on the West Coast. Lutherans have two important teachings about Baptism and the Lord's Supper: baptismal regeneration and the real presence.

Baptismal regeneration means just what you'd think it would mean: Baptism regenerates, makes new, or, literally, is a second birth—

as Jesus tells Nicodemus in John 3. Baptism isn't just a symbol or a proclamation of faith. Baptism does show the congregation that the individual is being brought into the Church, and this is an important thing, but it's not the entire point of Baptism.

Baptism forgives sin. Not because we do anything in Baptism—a common misunderstanding of how we think about Baptism—but instead because Jesus has attached His all-creative, world-making and remaking Word to it. All your sins—not just your original sin, not just the sin you have committed up until that point, but all of them, original and actual, past, present, and even future—they are all forgiven at the font of Baptism.

Baptism also brings a person into salvation and into the Church. This is the second birth through water and the Word that Jesus promises will save (John 3:5). It's an adoption into the family of God. Although we were born into sinfulness and lawlessness, enemies of God and our fellow man, in Baptism, this old you is wiped away, forever forgotten from the mind of God. Instead, you are given a new name: you are *Christened*, to co-opt an old word, with the name of Jesus and are now a beloved and redeemed child of God.

The Old Testament points us forward to Baptism, foreshadowing this divinely instituted washing. Consider when Elisha directs Naaman, the Syrian military commander who had contracted leprosy, to wash himself seven times in the Jordan River. Now, there was nothing special about the Jordan River—it's a shallow river, not much different from any other river. This is why Naaman initially balks at Elisha's instructions; surely Syria has better and more pleasant rivers (2 Kings 5:11–12)!

But it isn't the Jordan River that cleanses Naaman's leprosy—it's the word of God, given to him through Elisha the prophet, which Naaman receives in faith, even if he doesn't fully understand it.

Just like the Jordan's waters fully cleansed Naaman's leprosy, now the waters of Baptism cleanse us fully of the disease of our sin—not because of something we did or some magical property of the water but because Jesus has joined His powerful Word to the water for the remission of sins. Jesus instituted the Sacrament of Baptism as part of the Great Commission, when He told His disciples, "Go therefore and make disciples of all nations, baptizing them in the name of the Father and of the Son and of the Holy Spirit" (Matthew 28:19). Not long afterward, in the beginning of the Book of Acts, the apostle Peter says in his sermon at Pentecost, "Repent and be baptized every one of you in the name of Jesus Christ for the forgiveness of your sins, and you will receive the gift of the Holy Spirit. For the promise is for you and for your children and for all who are far off, everyone whom the Lord our God calls to Himself" (Acts 2:38–39). Baptism is a free gift from Jesus Himself—not an act of obedience on your part. It is an outpouring of God's love, bound to the waters through His Word, to free you from sin and bring you into eternal life.

This is why the Lutheran Church has always baptized babies and also why the Lutheran Church accepts Baptism by immersion, sprinkling, or pouring as all equally valid, so long as the individual was baptized with water into the triune name of God: "In the name of the Father and of the Son and of the Holy Spirit." Baptism isn't about you; it's not about your desire to follow God, it's not about your head knowledge or prayer life or devotional practice, it's not about you telling God and everybody that you want to follow Jesus. It's about Jesus picking *you*, through the means of the water, the Word, and the pastor or Christian doing the Baptism. Just because it happens through physical means, bounded by time and location, doesn't mean it isn't a work of God. The only way that God *can* work in our lives is by invading "human time"; even "spiritual breakthroughs" that happen outside of means, seemingly, are really through means—they happen at a time and a place, usually under the influence of people we know, books we've read, or sermons we've heard preached. Even prayer made within your heart isn't purely spiritual since it happens in time and within your heart, which is both spiritual *and* physical, a product of the union of your soul with your body.

I wasn't baptized Lutheran. I was baptized at age seven. I have two very clear memories about my Baptism: the first was that I was thoroughly convinced that I was doing it as an outward sign to God and the church that I had made a decision to accept Jesus into my heart.

The other thing I remember about my Baptism, though, in an ironic turn of events, became meaningful to me when I became Lutheran. I was baptized by immersion, but for some reason, right when my head was about to go underwater, I opened up my mouth to take a last breath and instead sucked in half a lung full of water. After what seemed to be an eternity, I was raised back up from the water, coughing and spluttering and embarrassed that everyone at church was watching me shoot water out of my nose. It's the closest feeling I've ever had to drowning. At the time, it honestly felt really anticlimactic. I'd messed up my moment in the spotlight! My time to show the whole church my commitment to Jesus flopped, with me a shaking, spluttery mess!

I returned to this memory a lot as I grew up. When my family became Lutheran, I remember initially being a bit confused about how they thought about Baptism, but over time, the idea that Baptism wasn't about my works, but Jesus' Word, and was all about His saving me and claiming me as a child of God—that idea sunk in and became a great comfort to me. At some point, my early memory of Baptism returned to me. Suddenly, a moment that had caused pangs of embarrassment for years became significant, and a bit funny too. Even in my youthful error about the nature of Baptism, Jesus still worked through it to save me. The water of Baptism, which I only thought of as a symbol, though it caused me to splutter and panic and think I was drowning, really *did drown me*, my sinful flesh and rebellion against God.

That old flesh in me continues to splutter and panic and kick, but I was truly raised out of that water, newly born into God's family.

Baptism is a wonderful gift, and it's all gift because it's not about what we do in it. But Baptism is a one-time gift. Jesus doesn't say you need to be born again a third, fourth, fifth, sixth time—just the one second birth of Baptism. Besides, since it's all about Christ's work and presence in His Word in the waters of Baptism, it wouldn't make sense to keep doing it. Jesus' Word is efficacious; it does what He says it does. Even if you're like me and were baptized at a time when you rejected the regenerative gift of Baptism, it is still yours. So long as you had a valid Baptism, with the Triune name attached to water, God used that time to begin working faith in you. And the faith that was begun in me in Baptism reached its culmination in realizing that I was, in fact, wrong about my Baptism! Hopefully you never had to experience that if you were baptized as a baby in the Lutheran Church. But still, from that moment on, the Holy Spirit dwells in you, working faith unto good works and pointing you back to Jesus.

But finding assurance would be difficult if Jesus gave us a one-time gift that we couldn't repeat and that was it. So He also gave us a gift that we can experience again and again and again: the Lord's Supper.

Lutherans have a very different, and as a result very controversial, way of understanding the Lord's Supper. Catholics teach that it is an act of sacrifice performed by the priest on behalf of the people. Other Protestants generally teach that it is a symbolic meal of remembrance, or they might teach that Jesus is spiritually present or that we spiritually ascend to Christ's presence in heaven in the Lord's Supper. Lutherans don't teach any of these ways of understanding the Lord's Supper. Instead, we teach the real presence.

Real presence is another one of those self-explanatory terms: it means that Jesus is *really present* in the Supper. What does that mean? Well, as we talked about earlier, Jesus is both God and man, spiritual and physical. In chapter one, we talked about distinguishing between these two natures in Christ without dividing His person. What that means is that, wherever Jesus is present physically, or as a man, He is also present spiritually, or as true God. Likewise, wherever Jesus is present in spirit, or as God, He is also dwelling physically, as a man. Because of this, the Lutheran Church has always taught that Jesus is fully present in the bread and the wine in the Lord's Supper. But since Jesus doesn't tell us how He is present, nor does He indicate that the bread and wine cease to be, unlike the Roman Catholic Church, we do *not* teach that the bread and wine cease to be or are only there in their "accidental" or visual forms. Instead, we teach that Jesus' body and blood is "in, with, and under" the bread and the wine. In this way, the Lord's Supper is a lot like how Jesus Himself has two natures: the Lord's Supper is simultaneously 100 percent bread and wine, as well as 100 percent Jesus' body and blood.

How this works is a mystery. What we can say is that Jesus' presence does not have the same limits as a normal human body. For one thing, church services happen all over the world, often at the same time, and Jesus is simultaneously present at altars in Georgia and Germany and everywhere else, day after day after day, for the past two thousand some odd years. Additionally, we know that Jesus' presence isn't like a normal person's body because this is not a cannibalistic eating. It's not gross; you don't chew up and digest Jesus' body like you do a cookie. That's what the Romans and Jews accused the Early Church of doing, and we know that God, being a good and just God, would not command His people to do something like that.

But much more than that, we can't say. That's why the Lord's Supper is a *mystery*, remember? And it's not that Jesus is present in the bread and wine just for kicks. Jesus is present to *forgive you your sins and give you eternal life*.

This can be scandalizing to hear if you're not a Lutheran, and it can get sort of glanced over if you've been Lutheran for a long time. First of all, where do we get the idea that the Lord's Supper forgives sins? From the Bible—in fact, from Jesus Himself. The synoptic Gospels and 1 Corinthians tell us that, on the night when Jesus was betrayed, He took the bread and said it was His body, the wine and said that it was His blood. Why? Let's see what Jesus has to say:

> **Now as they were eating, Jesus took bread, and after blessing it broke it and gave it to the disciples, and said, "Take, eat; this is My body." And He took a cup, and when He had given thanks**

He gave it to them, saying, "Drink of it, all of you, for this is My blood of the covenant, which is poured out for many for the forgiveness of sins." (Matthew 26:26–28)

Jesus is sitting before the twelve disciples and says that this meal is "for the forgiveness of sins." That's certainly a bit confusing, definitely even scandalous, but also exceedingly direct. He's saying, in so many words, "I am giving you this gift of My body and blood, and receiving Me will forgive your sins!"

But could Jesus have been talking about His actual body, not the Supper? Or could He be present spiritually, rather than physically? Or maybe He's just speaking metaphorically, and He isn't there at all? Well, the rest of the New Testament doesn't really support those alternate readings. Looking at the Epistles, for example, the apostles seem to understand the Lord's Supper in this same way. Paul writes to the Church at Corinth, "The cup of blessing that we bless, is it not a participation in the blood of Christ? The bread that we break, is it not a participation in the body of Christ?" (1 Corinthians 10:16). Paul isn't talking about Communion as though Jesus is only there spiritually or as though it is only a symbolic meal of remembrance. Why would he say that it was a *participation in the body and blood of Jesus* unless He meant that Jesus' body and blood were really, truly there?

Because Jesus is really, truly there. Just as Jesus is one person with a human and divine nature, as we discussed in the first chapter, so also His Supper is one sacramental union of His physical and spiritual presence in, with, and under the bread and the wine. It's 100 percent Jesus and 100 percent bread and wine.

How? It's a mystery! One that we will never figure out. But an even greater mystery is what goes on when we eat and drink of this Supper: we are bound to the body of Christ. Jesus tells us, "I am the vine; you are the branches. Whoever abides in Me and I in him, he it is that bears much fruit, for apart from Me you can do nothing" (John 15:5).

But how do we do that? How do we remain in Christ? How do we become His branches so that we might be sustained? Through the Lord's Supper, that's how.

Communion is that dwelling in Christ, that participation in Him, that He promised us. It is where we receive the forgiveness of sins into our very *mouths*! It is where we are given the desire and ability to "bear much fruit" by first eating of the fruits of Christ's Passion!

But isn't this a weird way to forgive us? Forgiveness is a spiritual, not a physical thing, after all; you can't *hold* forgiveness. Except now, God has decided that you can.

Human beings are prone to a false belief known as Gnosticism, a big umbrella term used to talk about any system of thinking, conscious or not, that values spiritual things over physical things. Sometimes Gnosticism is an intentional, organized religion; most of the time, though, it's just a sort of "operating system," if you will, that bubbles up in lots of different contexts. Many Eastern mystic religions as well as indigenous spiritualities have a Gnostic bent to them. Even the imaginary religion practiced by the Jedi in *Star Wars* is Gnostic! To be sure, our bodies and the physical world have suffered from the fall: they are corrupted, grow weak, and break down. All things that live are fated to die until Jesus returns (more on that later). But they are not any more or less fallen than our spiritual selves; the physical is neither superior nor inferior to the spiritual. This is why Jesus hasn't just promised that you will go to heaven, a good but ultimately temporary place for the soul after death, but instead, all the dead will be raised, soul and body reunited, and the faithful will live again in eternity with God. This will be the topic of the next chapter, but it's important to start thinking about now because this reality is seen in miniature at the Lord's Supper.

We weren't at the foot of the cross during the crucifixion. We didn't come upon the empty tomb. We didn't walk to Emmaus and hear Christ explain the Scriptures. We weren't in the locked upper room, we didn't place our hand into Jesus' side, we didn't watch Him ascend into heaven. While this is certainly true of all Christians who came to faith after about AD 30-ish, we also can't deny that the physical absence of Jesus from our lives would make faith, hope, and trust difficult.

We are physical beings, and there is no denying that. We are also spiritual beings, though, meaning that though we are temporal and finite, we long for what is eternal and infinite. And so Jesus, knowing our needs of both body and soul, spiritual and physical, gave us a gift that is both. Jesus gives us

a presence that is both physical and spiritual in the Lord's Supper.

He breaks all the laws of time and space, physics and biology and chemistry, and makes His true body present in, with, and under the bread and His true blood in, with, and under the wine, as a real, immediate, touchable forgiveness that you can experience week after week after week until Jesus takes you home.

But there is still even more to the Lord's Supper—this truly rich and deep gift that Jesus has given to us.

The Sacrament binds us to the body of Christ. But it also binds us to one another. Communion is always a communal act—it's there in the word itself! The Lord's Supper binds us to the other members of the Body of Christ on earth, a proclamation of our unified confession about Jesus and where He can be found.

But a lot of people don't teach the same things the Lutheran Church does about a number of topics, especially the Lord's Supper. We are, sadly, not united in confession with a number of Christian church bodies. This does not necessarily mean that they are heretical; heresy means a teaching that so utterly undermines the Gospel of Jesus that it destroys the saving message and, instead, leads to hell. Examples of heresy include a rejection of Jesus' divinity. Groups that teach differently without being outright heretical are called *heterodox*, which means "a different teaching." Heterodoxy is significant because often these differences in teaching result in roadblocks being thrown in front of the spiritual life of the believer. A person who lacks an understanding that Jesus is truly present in the Sacrament, for example, may struggle with a lack of comfort or assurance of her salvation or may feel as though she is far from God.

For this reason, Lutherans practice something called "closed communion," which just means that in order to commune with a Lutheran church, you need to confess the same things we do about Jesus—namely, our need for Him and His real presence in the Sacrament.

Maybe this seems harsh. Many people have stories of awkward family interactions when someone was denied Communion at a Lutheran service. To be sure, this goes against how we tend to think of religion. In America especially, religion is seen as a highly individualized experience, one that can't be infringed upon from the outside by religious institutions or authorities. But that's not how Jesus Himself talks about religion, nor is it how the apostles saw it either. Paul tells us:

> **For just as the body is one and has many members, and all the members of the body, though many, are one body, so it is with Christ. For in one Spirit we were all baptized into one body—Jews or Greeks, slaves or free—and all were made to drink of one Spirit. . . . Now you**

are the body of Christ and individually members of it. (1 Corinthians 12:12–13, 27)

We are bound together in *one body*, namely, Christ Jesus. As such, the members of the body should be on the same page. If your feet wanted the body to sit down, but your arms wanted the body to go swimming, wouldn't that create chaos? So it is with the Church and with the Lord's Supper.

The Church isn't a collection of atomized individuals each doing its own thing. We are supposed to be in communion, a community of like-minded believers. We can't go it alone because, just like the parts of the human body, we are utterly dependent upon one another. Gathering around the altar is a confession of this interdependence and unity of spirit.

And if this unity is not actually there—if we are not in agreement about Christ's Supper or any other major points of doctrine—then we shouldn't pretend like it is.

And really, it's not meant to be harsh. It's not a condemnation of someone to ask that they not commune because they have different beliefs. In fact, it's meant as the opposite: it's meant to protect them from judgment for sinning against the Sacrament, sinning against the very body and blood of Jesus Himself!

For this reason, you were given a pastor. The office of pastor has sometimes been called the "steward of the mysteries," or, in easier-to-understand language, the guard over the Sacraments. Remember what Jesus said: whatever you bind on earth will be bound in heaven, and whatever you loose on earth will be loosed in heaven (Matthew 16:19). Because of the importance of the Sacraments, God put called pastors in place to make sure that no one is abusing or misusing them. Consider, too, what the apostle Paul says about those who misuse the Sacrament: in addition to the bodily illness brought upon the people at Corinth, they also brought condemnation from God on themselves (1 Corinthians 11:29–30)! This is why your pastor may ask visitors to cross their arms when they come up for Communion if they are not Lutheran, do not confess what we do about Jesus and His bodily presence in the Sacrament, or are living in open and unrepentant sin. It's not to single them out or embarrass or exclude them. It's for unity of confession, for good order, and to protect people who might partake of Communion wrongly.

At the beginning of this chapter, we talked a little about the ascension as a way to ask, "Where is Jesus now?" Let's return to that question. When many Christians ask themselves, "Where is Jesus now?" they are asking, "Where is Jesus *contained*?" Where is the physical body of Christ locked into place, just like you or I are locked into one place at a time. The thing is, though, Jesus' body *isn't contained*. To think of Jesus in this way is to set off answering the question on the entirely wrong foot. Death and the grave couldn't contain Jesus' body—why on earth would physics, or even heaven itself, be able to, then?

Jesus isn't contained anywhere. Instead, Jesus reigns. Jesus reigns at the right hand of God, His throne of power in heaven. Jesus dwells in heaven with the souls of those resting in His grace.

But Jesus also reigns wherever His Word is present. Jesus reigns wherever sins are forgiven. Jesus reigns wherever God's children are baptized and nourished with His very body and blood. Jesus reigns in your heart, in the Word, on your pastor's lips, in the font, and on the altar. Jesus reigns wherever He is present for you to forgive your sins.

Jesus Is Present for You

Jesus' presence in His Word and Sacraments changes everything. It is one of the most important distinguishing beliefs we hold as Lutherans, setting us apart from other Protestants on the one hand and Roman Catholics on the other. This teaching can sometimes feel like a burden because of the awkward situations it can cause, whether that's arguments with family or hushed "just go forward for a blessing" conversations pewside with friends. It can be especially hard on pastors, who may face confrontation and anger from guests who don't understand the Lutheran way of doing things.

But Christ's presence is not a burden, despite the hardship we may endure as a result of other people's reactions to our beliefs. Jesus dwells with us—with *you*—here and now, offering you pardon, forgiveness, and peace.

That can take a long time to sink in fully, so let's meditate on it here. We so often feel lonely and isolated—from ourselves, from one another, and from God. Maybe you still berate yourself for a life-altering sin you committed in the past. Maybe you have a friend or family member with whom you have never been reconciled. Maybe you have prayed and prayed and prayed and God just doesn't seem to give an answer. In periods of overwhelming isolation, illness, and tragedy, it is so easy to feel like you've got to face everything alone, like no one understands.

But you don't—because you're not.

God is with you. Not in a spiritualized, intangible, symbolic way, but in a real, present, active, touch-and-feel way. When you were baptized, Jesus' very own promise was connected to that water. Jesus came to you in a specific time and place and claimed you as His own. When the pastor announces the absolution, whether to the church as a whole or to you individually, it is the very voice of Christ proclaiming that your sins are forgiven, forgotten, never again to be remembered by God. When you come to the altar to take the Lord's Supper, you're not just remembering Jesus or getting a warm fuzzy feeling for doing something "spiritual." Jesus Himself is dwelling with and in you, knitting you to Himself and to the rest of the Church, the Body of Christ—those standing next to you; those separated by hundreds, even thousands, of miles; and those at rest in Christ.

Jesus comes to where you can find Him. He isn't locked up in heaven. He isn't hiding in secret,

waiting for you to work out the mystery for yourself. Jesus wants to speak to you, lay His hands on you, feed you His very own body and blood.

Whatever your struggles, your fears, your sadness, your frustration, Jesus has taken it upon Himself so that you can know His blessedness and rest.

Jesus' presence also changes what it means to come to church. You get to experience a preview of heaven itself in the worship service. Have you ever thought about that? The world lays such a heavy burden upon us, and so God has given us the ultimate refuge, the congregation of believers in His most holy and precious presence. Sunday morning isn't just the time when we tell God how thankful we are and how much we love Him—this is a part of what we do by speaking back psalms to God and singing songs of praise, but it's much more than that. Jesus Himself calls us to His Church around the temple of His Body. The people and even the space are made holy, as, just like it was at the crucifixion, the veil separating us from the awesome presence of God is pulled back, and we rest in the protection and mercy of the triune God, reconciled through the work of His Son, Jesus.

Jesus has come to the place where you can find Him: His Word and Sacraments. This cornerstone of the Lutheran faith can be difficult to wrap our minds around, and it can cause us heartbreak when it is misunderstood, despised, or thrown back in our faces.

But take your confusion and frustration to Jesus Himself, who bears all our burdens and comes

again and again and again to take them away through His dwelling in you through the Word and Sacraments.

Your Good Lord desires the quieting of your mind, the soothing of your body, the forgiveness of your sins, and the conquest over your death. And He gives that to you, into your ears, onto your head, and into your mouth, through His presence.

Where is Jesus now? In His Word and Sacraments.

CHAPTER THREE STUDY QUESTIONS

1. Is Jesus locked up in heaven after His ascension? Why or why not?

2. What does the ascension tell us?

3. In what way is Jesus present in Scripture?

4. If Jesus is present in His Word, why isn't everyone who hears the Gospel saved?

5. In what way is Jesus present in His Word in absolution?

6. What does Baptism do for us?

7. What does the Lord's Supper do for us?

8. Read 1 Corinthians 11:29–30. Why do pastors sometimes turn people away from the Lord's Supper?

9. How does Jesus' presence in the Sacraments affect our identity?

10. Where is Jesus now? Why is this important?

CHAPTER FOUR

WHEN IS JESUS COMING BACK?

"Come, Lord Jesus!" cries the apostle John at the end of the Book of Revelation, the final (and perhaps most widely misunderstood) book of the Bible (Revelation 22:20). And we join him in this cry.

Whether at the common table prayer ("Come, Lord Jesus, be our guest") or in moments of dire anguish and deep distress, we likewise call to heaven, praying that Jesus would return soon. But when will He? And what is Jesus going to do when He does?

Especially in America, end-times prophets and predictions have been very popular, especially in the past couple of decades. Part of this comes from a healthy sense of alert watching, which Jesus Himself calls us to do in the parable of the wise and foolish virgins (Matthew 25:1–13). And to be sure, throughout the past two millennia, Christians everywhere have wondered if they were living in the end times, from the apostle Paul to the Protestant reformers to us today. We see the hurt, injustice, warfare, sickness, and death that is gripping this world, the godlessness of our society, the depravity of our culture, and we long for relief. This hope in Christ's return is good for the Christian to feel.

However, a lot of the end-times "prophets" have also been driven by a radically incorrect reading of Scripture. A number of misunderstandings have cropped up about the nature of Jesus' return. While this topic seems rather peripheral, especially when compared to the pressing issues of Scripture like the divinity of Jesus and the reality of His atonement, topics which we've discussed at length in previous chapters, Jesus' return on the Last Day is still a vitally important topic for Christians to wrestle with. Lutherans have a unique way of understanding the end times and last judgment, focusing always on Jesus and His merciful work for us. This way of understanding the end of days, a topic that can be frightening to think about, brings a great deal of peace to an otherwise confusing and even scary topic.

Even though misunderstandings about the end times and Jesus' return may seem unimportant when compared to the big issues facing the Church and the culture,

many of the teachings popular among other church bodies actually obscure the reality of Jesus' love and sacrifice for us. So, even while we talk about the end of time, let us always do so "looking to Jesus, the founder and perfecter of our faith" (Hebrews 12:2).

Jesus Will Return at an Unknown Time

We don't know when Jesus is coming back.

Jesus Himself said that only the Father knows (Matthew 24:36; Mark 13:32)! So if Jesus didn't

even know, then we're not going to figure it out either.

That may sound a bit anticlimactic, but it's the truth.

Jesus Himself speaks about the end times shortly before His betrayal and arrest, in a long series of parables and prophecies in Matthew 24–25 and Mark 13. What to expect as Jesus' second coming nears can be summarized as follows:

> **The physical temple in Jerusalem would be destroyed and the Jews attacked by Rome within one earthly generation of Christ. (Matthew 24:1–2, 15–22; Mark 13:2, 14–20, 30)**
>
> **False christs will come trying to lure away the faithful. (Matthew 24:5, 11, 23–28; Mark 13:5–6, 21–22)**
>
> **Wars and rumors of wars, natural disasters, famine, and unrighteousness will abound before Christ's return. (Matthew 24:6–8, 12; Mark 13:7–8)**
>
> **Christians will experience persecution, but God will not abandon them. (Matthew 24:9–10; Mark 13:9–13)**
>
> **The Gospel will be proclaimed throughout the whole earth. (Matthew 24:14)**
>
> **The whole cosmos will be undone and remade when Christ returns in glory to gather the faithful to Himself. (Matthew 24:29–31; Mark 13:24–27)**

No one knows when Christ will return, but we should "stay awake," remaining faithful and looking forward to the return of Christ and the restoration of all things. (Matthew 24:13; 24:32–25:13; Mark 13:32–37)

The temple in Jerusalem was destroyed about forty years after Jesus spoke these words, during the siege of Jerusalem in AD 70. A Jewish separatist group called the Zealots attempted to rebel against Rome. Despite the Zealots' early success, the Roman army stamped out the rebellion by destroying both the city of Jerusalem and the temple. It's important to remember that Jesus is speaking simultaneously about the short-term prophecy regarding the temple's destruction *and* the long-term prophecy regarding the end of time and Christ's return. This is true of other apocalyptic parts of the Bible, such as the Book of Daniel.

Jesus speaks at length about the state of the world leading up to His second coming. He warns of false teachers claiming to be Him; reports of violence, sin, and fear; and the persecution of Christians.

Sound familiar?

Ever since Jesus ascended into heaven, we have been living in the end times and waiting for His return. These descriptions can be applied to every period in history in one way or another.

Sin has so broken our world, and the devil is so hostile to the saving message of Christ, that this has been and will be the situation in which we find ourselves until the glorious return of Christ. Of course, there is good news too. Through the Holy Spirit, Christians will share the Gospel—the Good News that Jesus, God made flesh, has come and died to free us from our sins and give us eternal life—until it has spread throughout the whole world. We are still sharing the Gospel with remote tribes in obscure corners of the world—and also with our friends and neighbors who have yet to learn about the God who loves them unto death and back.

And that God-made-man is coming back too. This universe will come to an end, only to be reborn, without sin and without death, heralded by the return of Christ. When Jesus returns, He will return as a judge—which we'll talk about shortly. But this return is a big deal, which means we shouldn't let it sneak up on us. Jesus entreats His listeners to "stay awake"—to keep it in the forefront of our minds that He *will* return, even if we don't know exactly when. And when He does, He comes this time to judge. This doesn't mean we should descend into paranoia and anxiety, but rather, we should remain faithful. We should continue to go to church, to read our Bible, to receive the Sacraments, to spend time in prayer. The Holy Spirit enables us to do all of these things as we patiently wait for Jesus' return.

It's worth pointing out that nowhere does the Bible say that we can predict the second coming of Christ. While Jesus does give us the short-term prophecy about the destruction of the temple in Jerusalem, that is the only one of these prophecies that is tied to a single, specific, historical event. Similar short-term prophecies are found in the Book of Daniel about the rise and fall of the Babylonian, Persian, Greek, and Roman empires

(Daniel 2), but, like Jesus' prophecy about the temple, the foretold event has already passed; it isn't speaking to current affairs.

Lots of people over the years have attempted to calculate when Jesus would return—and so far, they've all been wrong. For example, many people in the Middle Ages expected Jesus to return in the year 1000 because of the references in the Book of Revelation to a one-thousand-year kingdom, also referred to as "the millennium" (*mille*, Latin for "one thousand" + *annus*, Latin for "year"). St. John writes:

> **Then I saw an angel coming down from heaven, holding in his hand the key to the bottomless pit and a great chain. And he seized the dragon, that ancient serpent, who is the devil and Satan, and bound him for a thousand years, and threw him into the pit, and shut it and sealed it over him, so that he might not deceive the nations any longer, until the thousand years were ended. After that he must be released for a little while. (Revelation 20:1–3)**

Obviously, Jesus didn't return in the year AD 1000. But people have continued to try to use this and other passages from Revelation or elsewhere to calculate the exact date of Christ's return. These types of pursuits always prove to be unfruitful for two reasons. Most obviously, they fail to take into account Jesus' own words that *no one* knows when the second coming will be, not even Jesus during His humiliation; God the Father alone knows. That means that no amount of ingenious mathematics and never-before-seen Bible interpretation will get you the right answer. Additionally, however, it is a simple misreading of the text.

The Book of Revelation can be a tough nut to crack, especially if you try to read it alone or in light of what we hear from certain Christian groups or on television. But it's actually pretty simple: the Book of Revelation shows us Jesus at the end of time comforting His people.

This and other texts in the Bible that talk about the second coming of Christ and the last judgment are important to understand—and can be pretty disastrous when misunderstood. The Old Testament Books of Daniel and Ezekiel and the New Testament Book of Revelation are all considered "apocalyptic literature" within the Bible. This doesn't mean that the books are about zombies or a nuclear bomb ending civilization. The word *apocalypse* is a Greek word for "unveiling," literally, the unveiling of a bride at a wedding when she is presented to the groom. That's just what's happening in the Book of Revelation, too, which is sometimes even referred to as "the Apocalypse of John." At the end of—or better, the remaking of—the world, Jesus, the Bridegroom, and the Church (meaning all Christians everywhere), His Bride, will be presented in their fully revealed glory to one another. Consider this stanza from the well-known hymn "The Church's One Foundation":

Through toil and tribulation
And tumult of her war
She waits the consummation
Of peace forever more
Till with the vision glorious
Her longing eyes are blest,
And the great Church victorious
Shall be the Church at rest. (*LSB* 644:4)

This is a perfect image of what John describes in the Book of Revelation: beset by great pain, sadness, division, and grief, the Church—the invisible body of all Christian believers throughout the world and throughout all of time—are all longing to see Christ face-to-face, finally freed from sin and death forever. We struggle in this life against sin and darkness, both found in the human heart and at a cosmic, supernatural level: "For we do not wrestle against flesh and blood, but against the rulers, against the authorities, against the cosmic powers over this present darkness, against the spiritual forces of evil in the heavenly places" (Ephesians 6:12). This desire and hope will reach its fulfillment when Jesus returns at the end of time—which is a profoundly *good* thing!

But why didn't John just come out and say that? Well, for one thing, "apocalyptic literature" like Revelation in the New Testament or Daniel in the Old Testament was common in the ancient world, especially among Jewish and Early Christian audiences. For Revelation specifically, writing in this genre may have been a way for John to avoid censorship. John was the only apostle to die a natural death, according to tradition. It is widely held that John was exiled to the island of Patmos off the coast of mainland Greece, where he was placed under house arrest during the persecution of the Roman emperor Domitian. In order to avoid his letter being intercepted and destroyed by the Romans seeking to stamp out Christianity, he may have written his epistle in this coded, stylized way, which would have been confusing to the Romans who lacked this sort of literary tradition. So that "one thousand years" reference from earlier is not a literal number but rather a figurative one. One thousand is 10 × 10 × 10: ten is considered the number of completeness from the Hebrew perspective, and three is the number of the Trinity. So one thousand is *super* complete, a number of perfection. Thus, the one-thousand-year period is kind of like saying "in the fullness of time," or "when the time is right." When the time is right, Jesus will come again.

It's important that we don't approach the books of Revelation, Daniel, or Ezekiel, and the end times by extension, as a code to crack or a secret to discover. The real danger is that these apocalypse-hunters and self-styled prophets of the end times may, if possible, lead away even the elect (Matthew 24:24; Mark 13:22) by distracting Christians from the real Gospel of Christ.

For instance, some groups teach that God works through many "dispensations," or ways of saving people, across history. Some such teachers and preachers argue, for example, that the temple in Jerusalem will be rebuilt and the Old Testament system of sacrificing animals will be reinstated. They teach this because they view Jesus' death and resurrection and the creation of the Church through the Holy Spirit as "Plan B" or a sort of side-project that God is running, but the real, original plan is a geographically situated political entity known as Israel. The danger in this teaching is that it can result in the belief that people were saved *without* Jesus before the incarnation—for example, by keeping the Law—and that people in the future might also be saved *without* Jesus, by observing certain Jewish customs.

A good rule of thumb is that if someone tells you that some people will be saved by something or someone other than Jesus, that person is a false teacher and is, whether they know it or not, trying to lure you away from God.

To be sure, God's people in the Old Testament did not know the full details of the Messiah-to-come; they didn't know that He would be named Jesus or that He would die on a Roman cross. But there were plenty of other prophecies in the Old Testament that pointed forward to Jesus that they *did* believe in—and just like us, they, too, were saved by grace through faith in Christ. But while we look backward, they looked forward to the coming Messiah.

Jesus makes this point even clearer when He declares, "I am the way, and the truth, and the life" (John 14:6). Two important things are going on in this text. First, this is one of Jesus' several "I am" statements, found especially throughout the Gospel of John. While it may be less obvious to us, Jesus was very intentionally using language that mimicked the "I am" language in the Old Testament. When Moses asked for God's name at the burning bush, God replied, "I AM WHO I AM" (Exodus 3:14), or, transliterated from Hebrew, YHWH or Yahweh (Hebrew doesn't have vowels, so most English speakers add them to make the pronunciation more obvious). Jesus echoes this language in order to establish His claims to divinity: when He tells the Pharisees, "Before Abraham was, I am" (John 8:58), Jesus very pointedly uses the same language as God used to identify Himself to Moses, language that the Pharisees definitely recognized, which is why they tried to stone Him for blasphemy. Jesus also uses this language to show the continuity between Him and the Old Testament. Jesus isn't bringing a new religion or a new "dispensation" through which God will save non-Jews. No—

Israel of the Old Testament was saved through faith looking *forward* to the *coming* Messiah—Yahweh come to save them from their sins—just like we are saved through faith looking *back* to the *risen and ascended* Messiah.

People who believe that God will reestablish a theocratic Israel with a temple sacrificial system simply miss this continuity between the Old and New Testaments. In fact, a lot of the

confusion about the end times and what it's all about ultimately comes from problems in how we read Scripture. Figuring out how to read the Bible is a challenge that has recurred again and again throughout church history, but it's another good example of something we can learn about by returning to the Reformation and Martin Luther.

Luther was frustrated by a couple of things going on in the medieval Roman Catholic Church. For one thing, the common people were not able to read the Bible because most people could not read Latin. But for those who could read Latin, they couldn't actually *understand* the text they were reading. The Bible is a long book, comprising different genres of texts, including poetry, songs, and prose. Some texts are literal, like the creation and the crucifixion accounts, while others are full of imagery and poetic language that needs unpacking, like the Books of Proverbs, Song of Solomon, Daniel, and Revelation. Sometimes, Scripture seems to contain contradictory messages or is unclear as to whom a text is addressed to. Additionally, a lot of words in Scripture can seem vague, technical, or confusing, especially when you are trying to read a two-thousand-year-old text written in a language you can't read and are relying on a translation. And don't forget about what we said in the previous chapter: to nonbelievers, the Bible is a closed book because it is only by the work of the Holy Spirit that we can believe (see Luther's Small Catechism, explanation of the Third Article of the Apostles' Creed). It's no wonder that Luther was frustrated!

We can borrow two sets of categories from Luther and our other forefathers in the faith to help us make better sense of the Scriptures: the first is clear versus unclear, and the second is Law and Gospel.

The easiest categories to use when trying to figure out what is going on in the Bible are *clear* and *unclear*. We should always consider unclear texts in light of clear texts, meaning that if we get stuck on a tricky and vague passage of Scripture, we should try to find a clearer passage about the same or a similar topic elsewhere in the Bible. For example, maybe you have heard someone talk about a "secret rapture," which is the belief that God will spirit away all the Christians from the world before He returns, leaving all the non-Christians to wonder why their friends, neighbors, and loved ones have vanished into thin air.

This teaching is drawn from a confusing and unclear text in Matthew:

> **For as in those days before the flood they were eating and drinking, marrying and giving in marriage, until the day when Noah entered the ark, and they were unaware until the flood came and swept them all away, so will be the coming of the Son of Man. Then two men will be in the field; one will be taken and one left. Two women will be grinding at the mill; one will be taken and one left. (Matthew 24:38–41)**

This text is a bit confusing. It is not abundantly clear from this text alone which is which: is the Christian the one taken or the one left behind? There are two ways to understand this unclear text through clear ones. For starters, we can reread the account of the flood in the Book of Genesis. Jesus is comparing the end times to the flood, so what happened in the flood? It's pretty clear:

> **Then the Lord said to Noah, "Go into the ark, you and all your household, for I have seen that you are righteous before Me in this generation." . . . The waters prevailed above the mountains, covering them fifteen cubits deep. And all flesh died that moved on the earth, birds, livestock,**

> **beasts, all swarming creatures that swarm on the earth, and all mankind. (Genesis 7:1, 20–21)**

In the flood, who was taken and who was left? Noah's family—the righteous remnant—were actually the ones who *remained*. God protected and sustained them through the ark, while those who had rejected God were taken away by the waters of the flood.

Additionally, we have other parts of Scripture that refute the idea that God will carry out any aspect of the end times sneakily. Consider this passage, just a couple of paragraphs up from the text in question:

> **Then will appear in heaven the sign of the Son of Man, and then all the tribes of the earth will mourn, and they will see the Son of Man coming on the clouds of heaven with power and great glory. And He will send out His angels with a loud trumpet call, and they will gather His elect from the four winds, from one end of heaven to the other. (Matthew 24:30–31)**

From this text, it's pretty clear that God won't be sneaking anyone away. When Jesus comes back, everybody will know, as He will return with "a loud trumpet call" and "power and great glory." Nothing secret about that!

So, even though that text about people being taken and left is a bit confusing, and you can even see

how someone might get the idea that the "secret rapture" is correct, we should never base a teaching on an unclear text. Instead, we should check that text against clearer texts to make sure that we have got the correct idea.

For this reason, we generally don't base whole doctrines around something we can find only in the Book of Revelation, for example. Revelation is such a complicated and confusing book, full of poetic language and apocalyptic imagery. It is still the inspired, true, and infallible Word of God, but it's not the best book to use as the basis for a major teaching.

The second set of categories gives us another important key to understanding the Bible and comes in handy in correctly understanding the end times. Luther and his fellow reformers stressed the importance of using these categories when reading Scripture, a tradition that has continued down to our modern Lutheran churches. The Apology of the Augsburg Confession, one of the primary documents in our Lutheran Confessions, the book of theological writings that Lutherans use to capture what we believe the Bible teaches, puts it this way:

> **All Scripture ought to be distributed into these two principal topics: the Law and the promises [or Gospel]. For in some places Scripture presents the Law, and in others the promises about Christ. In other words, in the Old Testament,**

Scripture promises that Christ will come, and it offers, for His sake, the forgiveness of sins, justification, and life eternal. Or in the Gospel, in the New Testament, Christ Himself (since He has appeared) promises the forgiveness of sins, justification, and life eternal. (Article IV, paragraph 5)

The Gospel always points us to Christ. Throughout Scripture, we find plenty of Gospel outside of Matthew, Mark, Luke, and John—even in the Old Testament! The saints and patriarchs of the Old Testament were looking *forward* to Jesus, just like we look *back*. The Law points us to the will of God, especially His will for how we ought to live in relation to Him and to one another. After the fall, we are unable to keep the Law—we sin when we break God's Law. The Law shows us our sin so that we would look to Christ, but the Law also acts as a curb for society, which is why all civilizations have similar legal regulations against things like murder and theft. Additionally, as Christians, the Law shows us how we ought to live, a goal that, though we will not attain it before Christ returns, we can strive toward with the help of the Holy Spirit.

If we look at the prophecies about the end times, the categories of Law and Gospel can help us avoid stumbling into error by trying to discern what we need to do to bring about the end times. Simply

put, we can't do anything to bring about Jesus' second coming.

The Bible's word on the end times is actually *Gospel, not Law*. Some people act as though we have to do something, usually some intervention into world affairs or other specific action, to bring about Jesus' return. But the Bible's description of the glorious reign of Christ is not something that *we* have to do or bring about. It's a *promise* that Jesus will return to raise the dead and save the faithful, and also that He is already reigning through His Church.

We cannot predict the coming of Jesus by studying current events. The Bible's prophecies about the end times don't correlate with our current political or military situations. Jesus Himself says, "But concerning that day and hour no one knows, not even the angels of heaven, nor the Son, but the Father only" (Matthew 24:36; see also Mark 13:32). If *Jesus* didn't know, we're not going to know ahead of time either. We should still be watchful, though, waiting in patient anticipation for the return of Christ. Because even if we don't know when Christ's return will be, we know that it will be good news for the children of God.

Jesus Will Return to Judge the Living and the Dead

We don't know when Jesus will return, but we do know that He will return and what will happen when He returns: He will return to judge both the living and the dead. The message of Christ's return is good news for us because it's a proclamation that Jesus, God-for-us, is returning to save us from death and the devil.

Even though the second coming seems scary, it's actually good news for Christians. Most people don't look forward to the end of the world—after all, it reminds us that we are mortal, that we will die. Unless Jesus returns first, we all will one day die.

Imagining death, let alone the end of the world, can be scary enough, whether our flawed and inaccurate cultural images or the prophetic language found in the Bible. But as Christians, we need not fear death or the end of the world because we do not need to fear the wrath of God.

More likely than not, you have experienced the death of a friend or family member. Even the death of a pet, an animal on the roadside, or a fictional character depicted in a book or film can affect us in a deeply emotional way. Make no mistake: death is horrible, absolutely and utterly *bad*. Any attempt by the culture to call death a "part of life" or "natural," though perhaps well-intentioned in some cases, is woefully misguided. Death was never a part of God's plan for His creation. Death is so awful because it is, quite literally, a curse. Death is the curse we fell into for rebelling against God (Genesis 3).

As Christians, we own up to the horribleness of death—but we also know that it's not the end. We are promised that, if we do die before Jesus returns, He will comfort us after death (see Luke 16:25; Revelation 7:16–17). And we don't need to fear the second coming because we don't need to fear what comes after that—the last judgment.

Jesus describes the last judgment in Matthew's Gospel. It is worth considering the passage here:

> **When the Son of Man comes in His glory, and all the angels with Him, then He will sit on His glorious throne. Before Him will be gathered all the nations, and He will separate people one from another as a shepherd separates the sheep from the goats. And He will place the sheep on His right, but the goats on the left. Then the King will say to those on His right, "Come, you who are blessed by My Father, inherit the kingdom prepared for you from the foundation of the world. For I was hungry and you gave Me food, I was thirsty and you gave Me drink, I was a stranger and you welcomed Me, I was naked and you clothed Me, I was sick and you visited Me, I was in prison and you came to Me." Then the righteous will answer Him, saying, "Lord, when did we see You hungry and feed You, or thirsty and give You drink? And when did we see You a stranger and welcome You, or naked and clothe You? And when did we see You sick or in prison and visit You?" And the King will answer them, "Truly, I say to you, as you did**

it to one of the least of these My brothers, you did it to Me."

Then He will say to those on His left, "Depart from Me, you cursed, into the eternal fire prepared for the devil and his angels. For I was hungry and you gave Me no food, I was thirsty and you gave Me no drink, I was a stranger and you did not welcome Me, naked and you did not clothe Me, sick and in prison and you did not visit Me." Then they also will answer, saying, "Lord, when did we see You hungry or thirsty or a stranger or naked or sick or in prison, and did not minister to You?" Then He will answer them, saying, "Truly, I say to you, as you did not do it to one of the least of these, you did not do it to Me." And these will go away into eternal punishment, but the righteous into eternal life. (Matthew 25:31–46)

Perhaps this passage seems upsetting or intimidating to you. Maybe you're trying to remember the last time you clothed the naked or fed a starving person. But the important thing here is that the works Jesus describes in this passage *flow out from the two groups' identities*: sheep and goats. Think of it this way: if you went out into a field and started baa-ing and eating grass and put on a wool fleece, we wouldn't call you a sheep. Sure, you're doing "sheep things," but it isn't doing sheep things that makes something a sheep. Instead, a critter that is *already a sheep* does sheep things, like baa and eat grass and have a fleece. The way something or someone acts is determined by what it or he or she *is,* not the other way around.

So back to the words of Christ.

The sheep—Christians—aren't sheep because they did good works; they did good works because they are sheep—Christians—and that's just what it means to be a sheep. Likewise, the goats—those people who reject Christ—are not cast out because of their works. Rather, because of their identity as goats—removed from Christ and in unrepentant rebellion against God—they cannot please God.

The sheep, those who trust in Christ to redeem them, receive their redemption. They join Jesus in everlasting life. The goats, those who rejected Christ, receive their rejection. They are cast out of God's presence in everlasting punishment. The redeemed go bodily to the new heavens and new earth; the reprobate go bodily to hell.

This is a hard teaching. It makes us very uncomfortable to be forthright about it. There will be people who go to hell and suffer for eternity. That's *terrifying*. Why would a good, loving God allow that?

God is actually allowing people to get what they want. To be sure, we do not *choose* heaven; the Bible tells us again and again that God chooses us through the Holy Spirit, who enlivens us to have faith in Him, and that our names are written in His Book of Life. Consider what John tells us: "If anyone's name was not found written in the book of life, he was thrown into the lake of fire" (Revelation 20:15). This isn't an arbitrary thing, and it also isn't as though God condemns people just to condemn them. Hell, as we said earlier, was originally created for those angels-turned-demons who rebelled against God, who chose to separate themselves from Him. It was not intended for mankind. However, if someone chooses to separate himself from God, to reject His mercy and try to save himself, then that person is choosing hell.

Our God is a God of grace and justice. His justice makes it impossible for Him to abide sin and unrighteousness in His presence. But His grace causes Him to love every sinner. The only way for God to be true to Himself was to send His only Son, Jesus, to redeem us, to make us righteous again so that we could dwell with Him forever. Jesus carried the sins of every single sinner and suffered God's wrath on the cross. That solution satisfied both God's justice and His grace. With every sin paid in full, Adam and Eve and all of their children could be saved by God's grace in Christ Jesus.

Those who reject this solution, who reject their Savior, are asking to stand before an almighty God on their own merits. And they can't.

This is what it means to blaspheme the Holy Spirit (see Matthew 12:31). Blasphemy isn't saying a bad

or mean thing about the Holy Spirit, but rather it is rejecting His office as the bearer of the eternal Good News, the Gospel of Jesus. To reject the Holy Spirit is to reject the saving work of Christ and to place oneself outside of salvation.

This is why it is of such vital importance that we share this Good News with our friends, family, and neighbors: hell is deadly serious. People who reject Jesus as Lord and Savior will not go to heaven. Furthermore, they will be eternally separated not only from God but from all their redeemed loved ones. And hell isn't going to be some edgy nightclub or picnic for cool people. We don't really know what all hell will entail—and it is not helpful to dwell too long on that topic—but listen to Jesus' description: "Then the king said to the attendants, 'Bind him hand and foot and cast him into the outer darkness. In that place there will be weeping and gnashing of teeth'" (Matthew 22:13).

Being bound hand and foot in outer or utter darkness shows there is no fellowship in hell, only solitary confinement, absolute separation from God, an existence devoid of warmth, light, and love. Christ saw this fate awaiting all of us, and out of great and divine mercy, took it on Himself at the crucifixion to save us from it. Nailed hand and foot to the cross, hanging in utter darkness, Jesus suffered hell in our place.

And now, being saved, we look on those around us with those same eyes of Christlike mercy and

lead others to salvation by sharing the life-giving and saving Word with them.

In Christ, you do not need to fear hell, nor need you fear sin and death and the devil. They cannot hurt you anymore. You are in Christ, and nothing can ever overcome that. St. Paul writes, "For I am sure that neither death nor life, nor angels nor rulers, nor things present nor things to come, nor powers, nor height nor depth, nor anything else in all creation, will be able to separate us from the love of God in Christ Jesus our Lord" (Romans 8:38–39). Evil will never conquer good—in fact, evil has *already been conquered* by good! And Jesus gives us even more comfort to help still our lingering fears about the second coming and the last judgment. He's done that by already doing it.

Huh? What does that mean, that the last judgment already happened? Now, it's obvious that it hasn't already happened for us—Jesus hasn't come back yet if you're reading this!

But Jesus has already borne the entire judgment for our sins. Jesus bore the very wrath of God the Father Himself on the cross: all of the divinely righteous anger felt by God for all sin, from the beginning of time to the end, all of your sin, all of your friends', family's, neighbors', and enemies' sins, everyone you've ever met, everyone you've

never met, all of the horrible and wonderful people across all of history.

It was all poured out onto the King of kings, Jesus, the Christ prophesied for centuries and born of a teenage virgin in Bethlehem. As He carried the cross, the judgment was prepared; as His hands were pierced by Roman nails, the judgment was rendered; as He gave up His divine and human spirit—Jesus said, "It is finished"—the judgment against all of humanity was completed there and then, two thousand some odd years ago.

Jesus has already taken the full judgment for sins upon Himself. All your sins have been taken away by Jesus—don't take them back! The only way that a person can be judged by God is if he denies Christ's atonement and takes his own guilt back upon himself.

So don't do that. Rest instead in the promise that Christ has already suffered the judgment that you and your sins deserved and that it truly is *finished*.

One more thing is worth thinking about as we near the end of this chapter. There is the chance that Jesus will return while you are still alive—that you will see the dead rise and will also be glorified without ever tasting death. But there is also the chance that you will die before Jesus' return. And, either way, you probably have had friends, family, or fellow churchgoers you knew who have died in the faith—brothers and sisters in Christ who will be raised from the dead on the Last Day and will be shepherded into the new heavens and new earth, paradise remade, without sin and death forever.

The last judgment is coming. But, in Christ, you have nothing to fear. Your sins have already been judged when Christ was on the cross. You have already been declared righteous by your Baptism into God's holy name and blessed family. You have already been grafted into Jesus and His Body, the Church, through Holy Communion. The Day of Judgment will hold no wrath for you because Jesus has already borne the wrath you deserved. Take heart, and be at peace: Jesus' second coming is good news for you.

Jesus Cares for You When You Die

But what about in the meantime? What happens after a Christian dies but before Jesus returns?

We know a little about what happens after someone dies, but it might surprise you how much we actually *don't* know. In the Gospel of Luke, Jesus tells about a rich man and Lazarus. It goes like this:

> **There was a rich man who was clothed in purple and fine linen and who feasted sumptuously every day. And at his gate was laid a poor man named Lazarus, covered with sores, who desired to be fed with what fell from the rich**

man's table. Moreover, even the dogs came and licked his sores. The poor man died and was carried by the angels to Abraham's side. The rich man also died and was buried, and in Hades, being in torment, he lifted up his eyes and saw Abraham far off and Lazarus at his side. And he called out, "Father Abraham, have mercy on me, and send Lazarus to dip the end of his finger in water and cool my tongue, for I am in anguish in this flame." But Abraham said, "Child, remember that you in your lifetime received your good things, and Lazarus in like manner bad things; but now he is comforted here, and you are in anguish. And besides all this, between us and you a great chasm has been fixed, in order that those who would pass from here to you may not be able, and none may cross from there to us." And he said, "Then I beg you, father, to send him to my father's house—for I have five brothers—so that he may warn them, lest they also come into this place of torment." But Abraham said, "They have Moses and the Prophets; let them hear them." And he said, "No, father Abraham, but if someone

goes to them from the dead, they will repent." He said to him, "If they do not hear Moses and the Prophets, neither will they be convinced if someone should rise from the dead." (Luke 16:19–31)

This passage can be tricky to understand, mainly because some of it seems contradictory to what we are told elsewhere in the Bible. People in hell can't communicate with people in heaven—we are told elsewhere that the faithful dead are at rest in heaven (Hebrews 4:9–10; Revelation 14:13), and it wouldn't be very restful to be talking with people in hell! The dead do not communicate with the living either. The dead do not appear to us to send us messages—we don't even really know if the dead are aware of what is going on in our lives back here on earth. While their bodies slumber in the ground below, their souls are carried by the angels up to Christ, where they rest and are comforted—that's what is meant in the text by "Abraham's side." This is what we talk about when we talk about heaven—the noncorporeal realm of God where He dwells in majesty with the angels (who likewise are spirit-only, lacking the physical bodies we have).

Sometimes, Christians act like this is the end, though, like the final destination for the Christian is heaven, the body discarded and forgotten about forever. But that's simply not the case!

God created us body and soul—and that's how we are meant to be. The separation of body and soul at the point of death is *bad*—really, really bad, actually. So bad that it is literally the punishment for our fall away from God. Our identity as human persons is found in the fact that we are this incredible, intricate, not-fully-knowable combination of physical and spiritual, body and soul, corporeal and noncorporeal. We occupy physical space and physical time, experience the world through our five senses, and share those experiences with the people who are physically close to us.

Christians are neither Gnostics nor Epicureans. Gnostics and Epicureans were both ancient Greek cultic groups, but their teachings and general leanings have been passed down throughout the generations and can be seen across cultures and even religious groups. Gnostics essentially taught that the body is worthless and the soul is the ultimate good, whereas Epicureans essentially taught that the body and its experiences were superior to the soul, pursuing lusts of the flesh, gluttony, and other physical vices. Both groups ultimately pit body and soul against each other, two natures that God united into us as one person, one identity, that ought to be understood as intimately connected and both good, God-pleasing, and meaningful to our personal experiences.

God isn't going to leave you floating around like a beam of light or something, with no body and no experience of the physical world. This would be to undo the "very good" work of creation He did in making you. Instead, Jesus is returning so that you will be reunited, body and soul, to live in community with other whole, body-and-soul people.

The second coming isn't just about the last judgment: it's also about the resurrection of the

dead, when all the dead will be brought back to life, with bodies made new, and the faithful will go to dwell with Christ and all believers across all of time together.

We don't know a whole lot about what this restoration will mean, but it will probably look a lot like what Adam and Eve experienced in the garden before the fall: they were in community with God, with creation, and with one another, in fully perfect headship over the earth and all of its creatures. We will fully know and be fully known by one another and by God. This is what Paul means when he writes, "For now we see in a mirror dimly, but then face to face. Now I know in part; then I shall know fully, even as I have been fully known" (1 Corinthians 13:12).

This life is good. This experience of being human, a physical creature with bodily sensation and a soul capable of thought, emotion, and morality, is "very good" (see Genesis 1:31). It has been marred by sin and death, though. But it has been redeemed by Christ. Death, the separation of the body and the soul, is not an end, nor is it eternal. God took on human flesh in the person of Jesus so, at the end of time, He could return, still fully God and fully man, to restore you to your full humanity, this time without sin and without death.

Consider these words spoken by Job:

For I know that my Redeemer lives,
and at the last He will stand upon the earth
And after my skin has been thus destroyed,

yet in my flesh I shall see God,
whom I shall see for myself,
and my eyes shall behold, and not another.
My heart faints within me! (Job 19:25–27)

You will look upon the face of God and live. You, looking with your own eyes, hearing with your own ears, touching with your own hands. Whatever ailments of body or mind you had on earth, no matter how long they tormented you, will be gone, forever, healed perfectly.

And what about in the meantime, while we await this glorious resurrection? Well, even though heaven isn't the final destination, it is a really, really good "rest stop," and not just for those who have died. In fact, every time you partake of the Lord's Supper, you experience a little piece of heaven on earth. Maybe you can't see it—maybe your sanctuary is dusty, maybe the lights flicker, maybe your church is in desperate need of a remodel; maybe your pastor is a little off-key when he sings and has a tendency to stumble over words; maybe the people at your church are quirky and even, maybe, a little difficult—and yet, in the midst of all of this deeply limited, deeply flawed, deeply sinful and damaged earthly life, Jesus has mercy on you, to bring down His heavenly throne room and all of its heavenly occupants *to you*. This is why we say "with angels and archangels and all the company of heaven" during the preface before Communion

(*LSB*, p. 208)—because that's what's really going on! And not just angels but also all those people who are communing at altars around the world, people known and unknown to you, and all those who have died in the faith, the great saints of yore, the reformers, the pilgrims and pioneers and missionaries, the martyrs—and also the grandparents, parents, siblings, children, friends, coworkers, and neighbors who died trusting in Christ too. They are truly with you in this little slice of heaven that you get to experience here and now, and you will truly be reunited with them, body and soul, when Jesus returns.

Jesus Will Come Back for You

Jesus is coming back to answer every prayer, heal every hurt, and fully restore your God-given identity. No more sin, no more sadness, no more pain. Only perfection.

Most people face some major mental or physical weakness or illness at some point in their lives. For some, it only comes in later life; for others, it defines their whole life; for still others, it cuts their precious lives tragically short. It's easy for these ailments to become a key part of our identity. Sometimes, even though the cancer goes into remission, the limb or joint is restored to normal function, or the cycle of self-harm is broken, the ghost of the diagnosis lingers on. The fear that the addiction, tumors, or disordered thoughts could always rear their ugly heads once more and drive us back into pain and suffering remains. And even if the disease is conquered, nothing will give us back those precious moments of life that were taken from us. Nothing, except the Lord of Life Himself.

But unto you that fear my name shall the Sun of righteousness arise with healing in his wings; and ye shall go forth, and grow up as calves of the stall. (Malachi 4:2, KJV)

No matter how serious, upsetting, embarrassing, or chronic a problem, Jesus *will* take it away from you. When you are resurrected at the remaking of the universe, Jesus will leave that pain in the grave where it belongs. Jesus will answer every tear-filled prayer for healing in that instant. And then, finally, your identity will become fully aligned with God's good will for the universe and for you. You are not your diagnoses, your traumas, your afflictions. You are not even your sins!

Who are you? You are the man or woman whom Christ will raise on the Last Day. That is already how God sees you. That is already who you are. It will be fully realized, fully known to you and to those around you on that day.

When is Jesus coming back? We don't actually know—but we also do. We don't know on what calendar date Jesus will usher in the end of time, but we know that He is coming, and He is coming soon, to raise and judge the living and the dead, and to bring rest and renewal to the faithful. For now, though, we know that Jesus comes back to us every week in the reading of His Word and in His Supper, with His full retinue of glory and might, to reunite you here and now with the whole company of heaven, to strengthen and comfort you and encourage you on the journey toward the end. Fear not! Your Christ is coming to you—and while He might be an apocalyptic hero, all that means for you is mercy, renewal, peace, and restoration.

When is Jesus coming back? Jesus will come back at the end of time, when He will judge all flesh and bring restoration to His Church.

CHAPTER FOUR STUDY QUESTIONS

1. Jesus teaches us in Mark 13, among other things, to expect "wars and rumors of wars," natural disasters, famines, unrighteousness, false christs, and persecution. These have been true for Christians throughout church history, because the world is broken by sin and despises God's Word. How do you see examples of these in your own life? How do you see examples of these throughout history?

2. How should we understand the Bible's prophecies about when Jesus will return?

3. What two sets of categories can help us understand Scripture better?

4. Read Matthew 25:31–46. Who are the sheep? Who are the goats? Why?

5. Read Matthew 13:47–50 and Matthew 25:41–46. What can we say about hell?

6. Read Hebrews 4:9–10 and Revelation 14:13. What can we say about heaven?

7. Why are Christians neither Gnostics nor Epicureans?

8. **What happens "after heaven," when Jesus returns?**

9. **What does Jesus' return tell us about our identity?**

10. **When is Jesus coming back? Why is this important?**

CHAPTER FIVE

WHY DID JESUS DO ALL THIS?

Whether you are two or eighty-two, the question that plagues all of mankind is and has always been "Why?" Why was I born? Why must I die? Why did he or she do that to me? Why is life the way that it is? For Christians, we have another set of why questions:

Why did God create me? Why did God determine that I should be born in the time and place that I was? Why does God allow me and those I love to suffer? And, most significant for us right now, why did Jesus do all of this?

We have spent the first one hundred and seventy pages talking about Jesus' life, work, death, presence, and future. We have meditated upon the eternal Godhead before the creation of time, the cross and the resurrection, and the dwelling together of all creation with its Maker for all of the eternity after time. We have a lot to think about and a lot to process emotionally, as well. But it all doesn't mean anything if we don't consider the *why* behind Jesus, the reason behind His nature, person, and work. It's worth thinking about. Why did God do all this? Why did Jesus take on human flesh, die on a cross, institute His Sacraments, leave us His Word, and promise to return to judge the living and the dead?

There are two ways to answer this question. The first may seem like a gotcha moment: we don't know. Like we've said throughout this book, Jesus, being God, is above our understanding. You might think salvation could have been achieved through a less slow, messy, challenging way. Perhaps you have wondered why

Jesus chose to be incarnated right around the midpoint of the Greco-Roman civilizations; why not before, or why not after? Why not wait until the advent of photography and videotape or smartphones and social media? I have no idea; nobody really does. God's ways are inscrutable, and He chose to do things His way for a reason—but a reason not known to us.

Why did Jesus suffer on the cross knowing only some would be saved and not others? Why not just blow the whole earth to smithereens as soon as Adam took a bite of that fruit? Why even allow Satan to tempt Adam and Eve in the first place? Why not just obliterate Satan and the angels who rebelled right off the bat? Wouldn't that all have been easier? I don't know the answer to those questions either. God is all-transcending, meaning His ways and thoughts are not our ways and thoughts (Isaiah 55:8–9). God is also the Creator, who alone has the right to do what He wants with His creation and His creatures, and we really don't have the right to question His choices.

We do know that God is merciful, though, and so we can say that all of these tricky, sticky "why" questions likely revolve around some part of God's loving kindness and infinite mercy.

This leads us into the second way we can answer why Jesus did all that He did: He did it for you.

Jesus Did Everything for You

As Lutherans, we make a really big deal about those two words "for you." They're in the Words of Institution spoken at every observance of the Lord's Supper—Jesus' own words explaining what that sacrament is all about. Maybe your pastor has preached a sermon about how Jesus is "for you" or you've read a devotional or listened to a radio program or podcast about how salvation is "for you."

Sometimes, though, phrases can lose their meaning and significance, just like when a child repeats the same word over and over and *over* again.

It can be easy to hear "for you" and make it sort of general or symbolic—about everybody or at least, everybody who is saved. While this is true—Jesus came to save the whole world, after all, as any schoolchild who's memorized John 3:16 can tell you—it's also true and very, very important that you understand that Jesus also came to save you, specifically.

Let's consider both.

Jesus' love for the whole world isn't abstract, though, like ours can be sometimes. For example, maybe you "love dogs" or "love roller coasters." More than likely, you do not mean that you have met every single dog in the world or ridden on every single roller coaster around the globe. No, you mean that you *generally* love dogs and *generally* love roller coasters. You could probably imagine some hypothetical dog or roller coaster that would break your rule, that you wouldn't love—because the dog was smelly and mean-tempered or because the roller coaster was dull and poorly designed.

That's not how Jesus is. That's not what Jesus means when He says that He died to save "the world." Rather, when we talk about Jesus loving the whole world and all people, we mean that Jesus knows and loves everyone as an aggregate because *Jesus loves every single person as an individual*. Think about that. There's not one single person you could imagine, from history, your own life, or your imagination, who Jesus would not love, or for whom He would not die. From the greatest to the least, able and frail, young and old, historically significant and historically anonymous. No matter who you are, you are known and loved, uniquely, individually, totally, and completely by Jesus.

Let's think about it another way. Remember when Jesus says, "What does it profit a man to gain the whole world and forfeit his soul?" (Mark 8:36). You've probably heard that verse dozens if not hundreds of times. We usually think about it in terms of *not* pursuing worldly wealth because it can separate us from God. But what if there's another thing going on in this passage, as well? Think about it again: Jesus is comparing gaining the entire world, all of creation, and a single person losing his own soul—not all of humanity losing their collective souls, just the one person and the one soul. Jesus says, in effect, that the soul of *one person* is of greater value in the eyes of God than *all of creation*, all the gain that could be gotten from this universe. You, dear reader, your soul is worth more to God than everything else He's created. Humanity was the crown of creation, remember—God gave His image and likeness to human beings *alone*. Humankind is the dearest thing to God, but not just as an abstraction or a generalization. God *is* love, which means He has the capacity to love all of us, each as individuals, fully and totally and with an all-encompassing, all-surmounting love that is beyond anything we can possibly imagine. That "for you," then, isn't just a "for y'all," but it is also a "for you, individually, specifically, uniquely, you."

When Jesus was bleeding and dying on the cross, He was dying for the sins of the world. All of them. Not just the people who would end up going to heaven, not just the people who deserved it (in fact, no one deserved it!). First John 2:2 teaches that Christ's death atoned for *all sin*. All of it! Everywhere! Across all time! All the horrible people from history, all the horrible people from your personal life, all the horrible people you've never heard of—and all of the normal, not-so-horrible people who need a Savior too. Everyone, everywhere, across all time—even the people who would reject Him. Those who end up in hell aren't there because there wasn't enough Jesus to go around—there was more than enough redemption for everyone. Jesus bled for every single sinner, even those who rejected Him eternally. And He bled for every single sinner who would embrace Him too. It's overwhelming to think about, but it's true. And Jesus was able to do this because He is God. His absolute innocence and holiness meant that, as a sacrifice, He counted for all people and all sin.

But Jesus was also dying for *your* sins, your numerable, nameable, specific, unique sins, known only to you and to God—and even those sins you've forgotten and those of which you are unaware. He subjected Himself to the terrors of God's wrath in order to save *you*. The face of the Son of God Himself was beaten, bloodied, and bruised; all the while, the image of your face, redeemed by that very same blood, was imprinted upon His heart so that His face would be imprinted upon yours. Because Jesus is also a man, He can atone for your sins, your individual soul. And He has.

The same Jesus who took so much care and concern to call His disciples and followers by name—Peter, Thomas, Paul, Mary, Martha, Lazarus—now calls your very name too.

Some of my pastors over the years have made it a point to call people by name while distributing the Lord's Supper. "Molly!" he'll say, "Take and eat; this is Christ's body, given for the forgiveness of your sins." It's a powerful reminder that Jesus' love is wonderfully, beautifully general *and* specific. I can hear the pastor naming each of the communicants, as we are all bound together in unity as the Body of Christ—it applies to us all. But it also applies to *me*, Molly. Not "other people," not even simply "everybody," but to each of us, individually. To each and every single "me" out there, Jesus cries, "I am for *you*."

And He cries the same thing to *you*, dear reader. Consider Jesus' triple-parable of the lost sheep, the lost coin, and the lost son (commonly known as the parable of the prodigal son). In each of these stories, the character representing Christ (the shepherd, the woman, and the father, respectively) goes out of his or her way to find the one lost thing—the single lost sheep, the single lost coin, the single lost son—that could have been easily overlooked, easily written off, easily forgotten, easily abandoned.

But Jesus will *never* forget or forsake you. Just like the shepherd, the woman, and the father in these stories, Jesus pursues sinners relentlessly, never tiring or growing weary, never running out of patience and mercy for the lost ones. Because Jesus died—*for you*. And wander as you might (and trust me, we all do), Jesus will always look for you, always come after you, so that He can forgive you, restore you, and bring you back into the fold. Whether that wandering looks like a period of spiritual malaise or a period of outright denial of Christ, nothing will ever dull or divert Christ's love for you.

Our lives can be so incomprehensibly messy sometimes. We all crave some kind of stability, whether we'd admit to it freely or not. Everybody wants a sense that they are the same person on Monday as they are on Sunday, and every day in between. But the sinful, fallen world likes to snatch even the most basic stability—a stable sense of self—away. Everybody goes through these small (or large) crises—anytime a vocation suddenly changes; a major person in your life leaves, changes, or dies; or illness, tragedy, chaos, or heartbreak creeps or barges into your life. When even the most foundational part of our life—our families—can change in the blink of an eye, it's no wonder that things like sudden changes in our jobs, personal lives, or even just our daily mood can be jarring and distressing. But there is one thing that will never, ever change, no matter how unstable the world around you and your very own identity may be: you are saved by Jesus Christ. You are a child of God.

The Bible tells us again and again that nothing can change God's love for us. Nothing in all creation,

not even hell and all of its demons, can snatch you from Jesus' nail-scarred hands (Romans 8:38–39). Christ's love for you is unchanging because He is unchanging, the same absolute and unremitting Love for all of time (see Hebrews 13:8).

Jesus has promised to be with us always, come what may, until the very end of time itself (Matthew 28:20). We might not always see it. It may not always look like Jesus loves us and keeps us. But above the storms and evils of this life, no matter what may assail you, Christ Jesus, the Lord of Life Eternal, stands above it all and yet in our midst, commanding all to obey Him and calming us with the words of the psalmist: "Be still, and know that I am God" (Psalm 46:10). God alone has the final say over your soul and your fate. And He has already spoken: "It is finished" (John 19:30). Your separation from God, your rebellion, your life of sin and wretchedness—it's all done. Gone. Finished. God has declared it, and it is so.

Before the Lord's Supper, many Lutheran congregations sing the following section from Psalm 51:

Create in me a clean heart, O God,
and renew a right spirit within me.
Cast me not away from your presence,
and take not your Holy Spirit from me.
Restore to me the joy of your salvation,

and uphold me with a willing spirit.

(vv. 10–12; see *LSB*, pp. 192–93)

We talked earlier about how the ancient world thought differently about the heart than we do. While we think of the heart as representing emotions or irrational thought, the ancient world thought of it more as the center of a person's identity, the seat of self, the innermost being. It's more like what we mean when we refer to "the heart of the matter"—the core of someone or something. Jesus came to re-create you at your innermost being. He replaced your heart of stone with a heart of flesh, as the prophet Ezekiel wrote (Ezekiel 36:26). What does that mean? You are no longer oriented to all of your life by your sin but rather by your Savior.

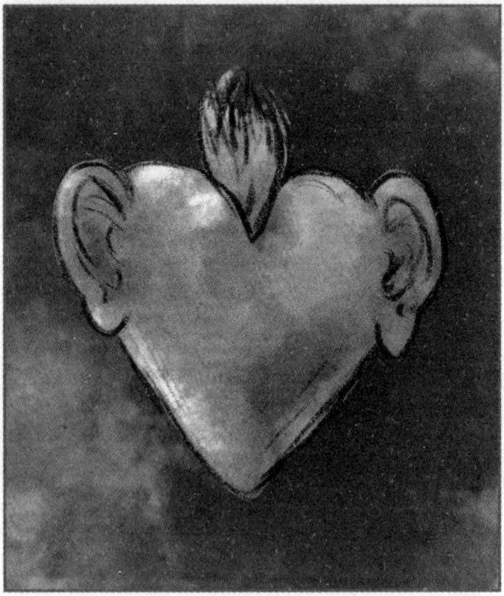

Some Reformation-era Lutheran church art shows depictions of the believer's heart with little ears. It's a really weird, surrealist picture—it made me laugh the first time I saw it!—but it makes an important point. Through His creative Word, Jesus made little "ears" on your heart, a heart that had been deaf to Him and His Word. Your heart—your whole being—now hears and responds to the Word of God, to Jesus, calling you to repentance and good works for your neighbor.

This ear-gifted heart has a mouth, too, a mouth to share the Good News of Jesus. Because Jesus didn't die just to save you—He died to save the whole world, all those precious but struggling men and women out there, hurting themselves and others in their separation from God. All those people across time and space, each one of them is a "you" for whom Christ died. As Christians, our job is to see one another through the eyes of Christ, to see each person in our lives as a Christ-redeemed, loved-and-bought-by-God "you." Each of your family members, each of your friends, each of your neighbors, each of your coworkers or social media followers or fellow shoppers at your local supermarket is a beloved son or daughter of God, bearing His image, for whom Christ suffered and died, with whom Christ longs to spend eternity. Christ chases after each of these lost sheep through you and through others like you. That doesn't mean everyone is a pastor or an evangelist or a missionary. Many times, we are the vessels through which God provides those around us with "daily bread," whether that's in the form of the food we grow or what we bring home from the grocery store or what we share with our friends. In every place where God has set us, all of our roles or vocations, God works through us to love the people with whom we come into contact on a day-to-day basis. It's not always impressive looking, and oftentimes it's hard, maybe not even what we feel like we really ought to be doing with our lives. Nevertheless, this is how God works through us to love others. And it works the other way too: God works through others to love us.

But, in the end, we always come back to Christ Jesus. Because even when you fail to share the love of Christ, even when you fail to take care of your neighbor in the ways you want to, even when you fail to fully grasp and express gratitude to the God-man who died for your sin, Jesus still forgives you, again and again and again. Jesus still looks at you as one of His precious sheep who He has redeemed through His precious and innocent blood. And so we return again and again to the cross of Jesus, this instrument of woe and wonder, where God Himself died for our sake—for my sake and your sake.

At the cross, we see the salvation of the whole world, and of you, specifically, as an individual too. But you can't travel back in time to first-century Jerusalem, and even if you did, odds are you probably would be a bit lost, unless you know ancient geography and ancient Near East languages pretty well. But that's okay because Jesus has promised to give us a way to reach back to the cross—His Means of Grace, the ways through which He delivers what happened at the cross *to you* here and now. God's Word is true, but it is also creative, turning simple water into a saving flood, bread and wine into His very body and blood for your forgiveness, and even turning the mouth of a humble man into a conduit through which the Savior of the world announces the forgiveness of your sins.

And because Jesus is for you, that means there is nothing else for you to do. You are freed from the unimaginable burden of your sin and trying to save yourself. You are freed from the slavery to

sin, death, and the devil, set free to God and to one another.

Your little heart, with the ears given to it by Jesus, cries out now, in thanksgiving and joy, to share that joy and blessing with others.

Jesus Christ Is Your Lord, Your Savior, Your Light

Jesus living, dying, and rising for you changes everything about your identity. Everything! Sometimes it doesn't feel like it, though, since we're so swamped by distraction and anxiety and things to do, people to see.

We're always busy, always going somewhere, always trying to get something done. It's hard to really contemplate Jesus' "for you-ness" when we're in such a hurry. So let's slow down.

Pretend for a minute that you're a peasant living in Europe around the time of Martin Luther. You probably can't read or write, you farm a little parcel of land you rent, and you have to walk or ride a horse anywhere you go. You probably don't own any books, or at the most, one or two. You don't watch movies or TV, listen to music on headphones, or scroll social media on your phone. You can't fill your home with pleasant and affordable art and family pictures. You have very little control over your situation. In fact, almost your entire life—your health, your physical safety, your food supply—is totally dependent upon God's provision for you through the weather, the cycle of the seasons, whether or not there is a volcanic eruption or sunspot or solar flare.

Every Sunday, and maybe other days in between, you go to church. Your time in church is like no other experience you have in the rest of your life. Your pastor and your church are decorated in beautiful fabrics, like nothing you own at home. You see beautiful paintings and statues of Jesus and biblical saints. You're told by your pastor that going to church is being in the actual presence of God—and you believe it. Your life can be so hard, so grueling, so devoid of color and beauty, so *dark*. But here, at font and pew and altar, your Savior, your God and Lord Jesus Christ is here—the once-dead but now ever-living Sacrifice to save your soul. And one day, though you will die and be buried, Jesus will grab you by the hand and raise you, body and soul, to live in everlasting goodness and righteousness, a whole universe re-created without darkness, without ugliness, without pain, without sin. And you, along with all the faithful from past and present, will live forever in that same presence of the Lord that you had at your little village chapel.

So, let's get back to you, reader, decidedly not a medieval peasant. Can all of this be true for you too? You probably don't live on a tenant farm, you probably have lots of pictures and art up on your walls, lots of books on your shelves, food in your fridge, conditioned air circulating through your home's vents. You've got TV and streaming music and more screen time than you could possibly want or need. Your life the rest of the week is stuffed to the gills with color and images and messages from everyone everywhere saying just about anything. It's all *so much*.

Whereas our premodern peasant friend's world sometimes felt like a desert, sometimes ours feels like a stormy sea, a nonstop onslaught of hyperstimulation, with the very foundations of our world—even our own personal identities—spinning and tilting like a carnival ride. We're all so busy, so stressed, so confused.

Can that Jesus who meant so much to the illiterate, uncultured peasant in the tiny medieval church have something to say to you too?

Yes.

One of my favorite services to attend in our Lutheran churches is Evening Prayer. I can't tell you how many times I've stumbled into an Evening Prayer service exhausted, frazzled, and positively burned out.

The weight of just *existing* some days can feel suffocating—the amount of things I need to do, the horrifying headline I read online, the stressful situation with a friend or family member I need to navigate, the nagging insecurity gnawing in my chest, the unkind thing I said earlier rattling around in my head. Who am I? What am I doing here?

Why did God even bother putting me on this planet if this was what life was going to be like?

And then everything swirling around my head stops because the pastor chants in a loud voice: "Jesus Christ is the Light of the world!" And I join the rest of the congregation in replying, "The light no darkness can overcome!" (*LSB*, p. 243).

The service continues on, a wonderful meditation on Christ's work to bring light into our darkened world. We're not actually different in any meaningful way from our peasant friend from earlier. We're all sitting in darkness. We're all groping around trying to find something to cling to in this world and not finding anything.

The thousands of voices screaming at us day in and day out will never bring us comfort—but that's okay because Jesus already has. Jesus is the Light that dispels the darkness of our sin, casting away the darkness that has crept into our souls and confused our minds.

And because Jesus is also your Light, you no longer have to keep searching for your identity or figure out what you're supposed to do. Jesus has already told you.

In your Baptism, Jesus told you the reason you were born: in order that you could become God's own child, a precious and miraculous union of body and soul redeemed by His blood. Every time you confess your sins, Jesus tells you that, no, you *aren't* supposed to sin—but that's why He died on the cross. And now, He sends you His Holy Spirit, so that you would be strengthened and enabled to resist temptation. Whenever you celebrate Communion at your church, Jesus tells you that He has placed you into this time and place to be with the other people around you at the altar rail, to serve them and encourage them in the faith, and that, one day, you will all be raised again to live in everlasting blessedness. All of this Jesus has made possible by being born, living, dying, and rising. Jesus, the creative Word and Light of God who spoke all light into existence, became a human man, *forever*, a holy and unfathomable mystery, all so that the light of His divine face could shine on you—*you*, dear reader, and all the faithful—to make you His.

Why did Jesus do all this? He did it all for you.

CHAPTER FIVE STUDY QUESTIONS

1. **How does God love us differently than we love things?**

2. **What does it mean that Jesus died for the whole world?**

3. **What does it mean that Jesus died for you?**

4. **Read Luke 15, which contains the three parables of the lost sheep, the lost coin, and the lost son. What is the running theme between all three of these parables?**

5. **Read Romans 8:38–39; Psalm 46:10; Matthew 28:20; and Hebrews 13:8. What do these verses tell us about Jesus and His love for us?**

6. **How has God changed our hearts?**

7. **How should we view the people around us?**

8. **What do we do now that Jesus has done it all?**

9. **What does Jesus' dying and rising for you tell us about our identities?**

10. Why did Jesus do all this? Why is this important?

EPILOGUE:

BRINGING IT ALL TOGETHER

Ever since I became Lutheran, I seem to have developed some kind of magnetic pull that drags me into what I call "awkward Jesus conversations," usually with people I barely know. They're never planned—hence the awkward!—like the time I had a two-hour conversation with a friend-of-a-friend I had just met about why mankind is in need of salvation or the time my German professor asked me to explain the difference between my Lutheran church and her state Lutheran church—in German!

One time, I was at my college's library picking up a couple of books before heading to class when I ran into a classmate—let's call him Steve—and Steve and I decided to walk to class together.

I was working on a project in class that involved the Reformation, and that led to a conversation about religion. Steve told me he didn't grow up religious and never had been, and then asked if I was.

"Yeah, I'm Lutheran actually. Missouri Synod, if that means anything to you," I replied. I grew up in California and then spent several years in Alabama, neither of which is exactly a Lutheran hot spot, so I usually expect people not to know what a Lutheran is, let alone the ins and outs of inter-Lutheran denominational differences.

It turned out, though, Steve actually knew what the Lutheran Church—Missouri Synod was because he knew someone who had grown up LCMS but left as an adult.

"Oh really?" I said, awkwardly. (How do you respond to that? I made a choice, quickly and nervously.) "I actually *became* Lutheran, around when I was fourteen. I had been nondenominational before that."

Now it was Steve's turn to be uncomfortable, and I grew increasingly nervous. Missouri Synod Lutherans are mostly known in the wider culture, especially on a college campus, for their beliefs about the sanctity of life and traditional marriage, neither of which would have endeared me to most of my classmates. In fact, the response I got from many of my classmates and colleagues in graduate school when they found out my husband was attending seminary was a confused, vacant stare. I'm sure that his (correct) assumptions about my stances on social issues informed what he said next.

"I'm just surprised, I guess," Steve said with an uncomfortable little cough. "Do you mind me asking . . . why did you become Lutheran, like, *Missouri* Lutheran?"

I'd like to remind you that all of this happened during a five-minute-or-less walk from the library to class. We were nearing the building, and I was running short on time. Not only that, but he had said he had *no* experience with Christianity—would a big diatribe on faith alone or the real presence or any of the individual points of doctrine that drew me to the Lutheran Church make any sense to him, or would they all just fly over his head? And what little I knew about Steve, I knew we were about as polar opposite on the political spectrum as you can feasibly get, and a political conversation would be radically unhelpful and distracting. I could feel a cold sweat forming on my back and the palms of my hands in the brief seconds that passed between his question and my answer, seconds that felt like an eternity. I blurted out: "Well, being Christian is all about *Christ,* right? I became Lutheran because the Lutherans talk more about Jesus than anybody else does."

I wish I could say that conversation blossomed into something meaningful, that Steve converted and I was his baptismal sponsor, or even that we resumed the conversation later and had meaningful dialogue. We didn't. He dropped the whole thing, changed the subject, and never brought it up again.

Most of my "awkward Jesus conversations" usually end up going like that. I pray they are meaningful for the other person in the long run, but they usually end anticlimactically for me, leaving me with a million words unsaid, a slightly elevated heart rate, and gross, sweaty hands—the picture of awkward.

This one was a little different for me, though. The words I said rattled around in my head for days after. What did I mean by that? Being Lutheran—being *Christian* at all—is all about Christ Jesus. What does that mean? And what does it mean for me?

The Church—from the apostles to the reformers to believers today—has thought and fought about who Jesus is. In fact, Jesus is still asking us, "Who do you say that I am?" (Matthew 16:15).

And sometimes, just like the apostles, we struggle to come up with a coherent and satisfying answer.

The best place to start when you don't know the answer is to think about the question. Who is Jesus? He is your Savior. What did Jesus do? He saved you. Where is Jesus present? In His Word and Sacrament, given for you. When is Jesus coming back? At the end of time, to raise you to everlasting blessedness. Why did Jesus do all this? He did it for you—to save you from your sin and the death and punishment you deserved and instead to give you His righteousness.

I studied German in college, and one of the things I enjoyed learning about in my program was the music and faith of Johann Sebastian Bach, the most famous Lutheran composer and one of the greatest musicians of all time. Bach wrote a piece of music called the *St. John Passion*, which is the entire Passion narrative from the Gospel of John set to music, interspersed with snippets of hymns. One of those hymn snippets goes something like this:

Within my heart's foundation

Your name and cross alone

Shine unto end of ages

A source of joy unknown!

You gaze upon me kindly,

Give comfort in my need;

To save me, Lord, You mildly,

Did suffer, die, and bleed.[6]

6 Author's translation.

This is it. This is what it's all about. We cling to Jesus Christ alone because of who He is, what He has done, where He is present, when He is coming back, and why He did all that He did.

Because that's what it means to be Lutheran. Because that's what it means to be Christian. Because it's *everything*. Because Jesus, true God, true man, came to earth to bleed and die in order to save you from sin, death, and the devil, to rescue you from the evils of the world and your own sinful flesh.

When Jesus spoke the words from the cross, "It is finished," He was talking about the debt *you* owed, the punishment *you* deserved, the death and torment *you* should have received. But "it is finished"! The debt has been paid, the punishment taken, the death and torment borne. It is no more! It is totally, completely, utterly, ultimately finished! Rejoice and be glad! Because the God who became man and died now *lives*! "O death, where is your victory? O death, where is your sting?" (1 Corinthians 15:55). Death can no longer claim you because Jesus has *destroyed* it. Sin, death, and the devil no longer hold the final say over your body and soul, over your heart, over your whole being, because Jesus has driven them out and reigns there instead. And there He will be, always with you, even unto the end of the age (Matthew 28:20).

In some ways, being a Christian can be complicated. The Bible is a challenging book to read. Law and Gospel can be difficult to divide. The mysteries of our faith can be hard to believe. Add on top of that the many attacks on our faith from the world, the devil, and our own sinful flesh, all of which fight daily and hard to break the grip of our Savior on our hearts.

And yet, in many ways, being a Christian is simple. It's all about Jesus. All of it. It can be all too easy to get distracted by the things in the world and in our own lives, easy to try to turn Christianity into a social club or a morality league or a social welfare program. But that's not what it's about; that's not what it means to be Christian.

Holding onto Jesus: that's what it means to be Christian. It means confessing Jesus Christ as true God, true man, and true Savior—truly *your* Savior. It means looking to the cross alone for your salvation. It means coming to the place where Jesus promises to be to forgive your sins, comfort your conscience, and give you life: His Church, in His Word and Sacraments. It means waiting for Jesus' triumphant return to bring the new heavens and the new earth, and until then praying, "Thy will be done; Come, Lord Jesus!" It means crying out, "My God, my God, why have you *not* forsaken *me*!" in sheer, tearful, grateful joy. And we will probably never fully understand. It's a divine mystery. Our everlasting Savior, holy Brother, perfect Friend, Jesus, has saved us from every evil and wicked thing in the whole of creation by taking it all unto Himself. Be at peace and confess Jesus. Confess Jesus as God and man, the crucified King, the holy Presence in His Sacraments, the Judge and Re-creator of all things. Confess Jesus as *yours*. Jesus is yours, and nothing can ever, ever change that.

STUDY QUESTIONS AND ANSWERS

CHAPTER ONE

1. **We talked a lot in this chapter about how Jesus has two natures but is one person. Using the examples and definitions on pages 18 and 19, define *nature* and *person* in this context.**

   A *nature* is a set of characteristics that defines a category. In this chapter, we read about the set of characteristics that defines cats. Feel free to consider natures for other easily characterized things. In relation to Jesus, Jesus has two natures: a divine nature (meaning He is God and thus has divine attributes) and a human nature (meaning He is man and thus has human attributes).

   A *person* is an individual essence or unity. What this means is that even though the eternal Word existed from eternity but was incarnated at a specific point in time, this doesn't mean there are two Jesuses. The Son of God remains unchanged in essence, and will remain both God and man forevermore.

2. **What are the two categories that divide the whole universe, and what differentiates them?**

   Creation is everything that God has made. It includes you and me, plants, animals, minerals, all natural phenomena, and supernatural beings like angels. All of these things are deeply dependent upon God and upon the rest of creation. Human beings are the crown of God's creation, because He has made us in His image.

   The Creator is the triune God, one in essence, three in persons, Father, Son, and Holy Spirit. He has existed from eternity, is not dependent upon anything or anyone, is all-powerful, all-knowing, all-present.

But most important, the true and living God is love, which is why He sent His one and only Son, Jesus, to redeem us by becoming one of us.

3. **What can we find out about God from nature, reason, and the world around us? What can we find out about God *only* from the Bible?**

   From nature, reason, and the world around us, we can tell that God is big, powerful, and angry. From the Bible, we discover His plan to redeem us through Jesus Christ.

4. **Other religions talk about human beings who became gods or who were "sons of gods." How is Jesus different from these mythological figures?**

   Many of the people who "became gods" were human political figures, like Roman emperors or Egyptian pharaohs, who used this title as a means of gaining worldly power and prestige. Many of the mythological figures who are referred to as "sons of gods" were actually demigods, meaning they were produced from the (usually illicit and almost always scandalous!) union of a human being and a god (like Zeus's many affairs in Greek myth). None of these figures claimed to be morally perfect or the savior of the world. In contrast, Jesus was both fully man and fully God. He claimed to have existed with God in the Trinity before the beginning of time. He claimed to be morally perfect and the promised Savior of the world.

5. **What can we learn about Jesus from the Bible? What can we learn about Jesus from history? What purpose do these two types of knowledge serve?**

   Looking at the Bible, we learn that Jesus is both God and man, performed miracles, and died and rose again for our sins. Looking at history can help us verify that the Bible gives us accurate information about Jesus. For example, historical sources support the Bible's claims that Jesus was crucified because He claimed to be the Messiah and one with God. However, history alone does not give us faith. Faith is found only with the Holy Spirit guiding us as we read the Bible and what it has to say about Jesus.

6. **Look back on page 32 for the (incomplete!) list of Old Testament prophecies and their fulfillment in the life of Christ. If you are in a group, give each person a verse or two to look up; if reading individually, pick a few that are of particular interest to you. What**

strikes you about these passages? What is the significance of the little tidbits from the early life of Christ?

These short passages from the New Testament, many of which we read over quickly as we try to get to the beginning of Christ's public ministry, all show that Christ is the Messiah foretold by prophets long ago. They help establish the validity of the claims He will make later, claims of divinity that serve as the bedrock of our faith. Furthermore, these passages also show us the true humanity of Christ, as He lived all those same human experiences we go through.

7. **What does it mean that Jesus has two natures but one person?**

Jesus is both the eternal Son of God, who existed from all eternity, and a human man born to Mary, with specific features, height, weight, voice, eye color. There aren't two Jesuses, but one, a unified person who existed before His incarnation but now forevermore has a body. Further, Jesus has both human and divine attributes. These aren't mingled or mixed together, but rather remain separate. Nevertheless, Jesus is able to use His divine nature in spite of the limitations that His human nature seemingly has, because He is God. Jesus laid aside His glory and power for a time, seen most fully at His crucifixion and death. Yet He also performed miracles, walking on water, healing the sick, raising the dead, and appearing in the locked upper room, among others. He was able to do all these things even though He is fully man because He is still fully God. And now, raised from the dead, ascended, and fully glorified, Jesus is able to do all things according to His divine nature.

8. **What are some of the ways that we get our human identities wrong?**

We often tend to swing between extremes of loving ourselves and acting like we are a god unto ourselves or hating ourselves and acting like we are beyond the love of God.

9. **What does the incarnation tell us about our identity?**

The incarnation tells us that we are not God—we are God's creation, fully dependent upon Him for all our needs. Yet we are also of incredible worth to God because of what Christ has done for us. Our souls and bodies are restored to and beloved by God, and, by the Holy Spirit, we are called to act accordingly to ourselves and to one another.

10. Who is Jesus? Why is this important?

Jesus is our true God, who took on real human flesh in order to save you and me. Jesus' incarnation makes our redemption possible and reveals to us the nature of God and His desired relationship with us.

CHAPTER TWO

1. Read Isaiah 53, a prophecy about the death and saving work of Jesus Christ. Meditate on it individually or as a group. What picture does the prophet Isaiah paint of Christ?

Isaiah 53 can be an intense and emotional read. The prophet paints Jesus as an utterly broken, scorned, wretched sacrifice. This depiction is difficult to bear and is hard to align with our ideas about how God should act. Instead, it shows us what Christ is willing to suffer on our behalf. Jesus bears the greatest shame imaginable—being tortured to death—in order to save us from our sins.

2. Read the following "I am" statements from Jesus: "I am the Good Shepherd" (John 10:11–18); "I and the Father are one" (John 10:30); "Before Abraham was, I am" (John 8:58). Why are these passages significant? Why did Jesus' audience become so angry with Him over these statements?

These passages all show that Jesus claimed to be God, the promised Messiah to save all people from their sins. When people heard these claims, they rejected Jesus, usually because they misunderstood Scripture or rejected a key teaching of the Bible. Jesus was not the Messiah or the God that they wanted, and so they rejected Him.

3. How does the Bible define evil, sin, and death? How are the three related?

Evil is a negation of good, a lacking or absence of what aligns with the will of God. Sin is an act of rebellion against God and His will for the universe, a destructive act of rejection. Death is the just consequence of sin, the sundering of body and soul. All of these entered the world through the fall, not by God, but by the failure of man to follow God's will.

4. In what way do we have free will? In what way do we not have free will?

We have free will in that we are not robots or marionettes whose every waking decision is dictated by God. You exercised free will to choose what clothes to put on today and whether or not to go to work, among other things. However, you cannot choose to do good or please God. You cannot choose not to sin. You have a bound will with regard to your sin nature, meaning you cannot save yourself.

5. **What does the Bible have to say about our heart? Why is that important? (Look at pp. 70–71 for a list of relevant Bible passages.)**

   The heart is the seat of our whole person and identity. The Bible uses "the heart" to talk about everything that a person is. The Bible also frequently talks about how defiled, hard, and God-hating our hearts are. This means that our whole person has been deformed by sin.

6. **What does substitutionary atonement mean? Why is it important?**

   Substitutionary atonement means that Jesus makes us right with God by taking our place and bearing the punishment we deserve. Some people claim that Jesus' sacrifice was a metaphor or a symbol or an example. Some people reject the notion that Jesus died on your behalf. All of these are direly wrong, because the Bible makes clear that we need redemption, and that requires a sacrifice. Jesus is the sacrifice to end all sacrifices, the once-for-all death of the absolutely innocent and totally Holy God on our behalf.

7. **Read 1 Corinthians 15:12–19. On what event is our faith based?**

   Our faith hinges upon the death and resurrection of Christ Jesus. If it were untrue, nothing would matter. Since it is true, nothing else matters more. Jesus dying for your sins changes everything.

8. **What makes Jesus' resurrection similar to and different from other raisings of the dead in the Bible, such as that of the widow of Zarephath's son or Lazarus?**

   These other raisings of the dead in the Bible all prove the prophet's legitimacy, as only God can raise the dead; Jesus raises the dead to show mercy as well as perform a sign that validates His claims to divinity. Jesus' rising from death is done without the intervention of a third party like a prophet, because it is also a declaration that sin has been vanquished forever.

9. **What do Jesus' death and resurrection tell us about our identity?**

   The death of Christ shows us that God loves us superabundantly. God Himself died to save you! In rising, Jesus proclaims that you, who shared in His death, will now share in His life. Your heart—whole identity—is made new, redeemed, perfected, and you are declared worthy to stand before the all-holy God.

10. What did Jesus do? Why is this important?

Jesus died to save you. You were dead in your sins, unable to save yourself, condemned to hell and life forever apart from God. But Jesus took away this punishment, paid for your sins, and gives you His everlasting life and blessedness in exchange.

CHAPTER THREE

1. Is Jesus locked up in heaven after His ascension? Why or why not?

No, He isn't. Jesus is fully man and fully God, which means that, after His resurrection, He is no longer limited by the laws of physics as they would pertain to a normal human body. He is able to do many things that would be impossible for any of us, like disappear, walk through walls, heal the sick, and, now, be present both in heaven and on earth.

2. What does the ascension tell us?

The ascension proclaims Jesus' total victory over sin and death. It tells us that His period of humiliation is over, and now He is fully exalted, able to do all things for us. Jesus' ascension into heaven is a triumphal entry that shows the whole universe that He is King of all.

3. In what way is Jesus present in Scripture?

Jesus is the living and active Word of God. The Bible is this same Word of God, which creates saving faith. Scripture both tells us about God and brings us the presence of God. This is also true of other contexts where Scripture is spoken or repeated, such as the hymns and liturgy we sing and hear in church. Jesus is truly present wherever His Word is proclaimed.

4. If Jesus is present in His Word, why isn't everyone who hears the Gospel saved?

Ultimately, we cannot answer the question of why some are saved but not others in a complete and perfect way. What we do know is that God does predestine those who are saved—Jesus has chosen you from eternity to be His baptized child. However, God does not predestine damnation, meaning He doesn't pick out who is going to reject Him and go to hell. Those who reject God are doing so of their own accord and of their own will, choosing the eternal separation that they receive. This is a paradox that we cannot ever fully comprehend. Nevertheless, we should continue to share His Word with those around us, even those who have previously rejected Jesus.

5. In what way is Jesus present in His Word in absolution?

Jesus promises that pastors will act as His proxies on earth, binding and loosing sins in accordance with His will. When your pastor forgives your sins corporately or individually, Jesus speaks, acts, and forgives through him. The words of absolution you hear from your pastor are just as if Jesus Himself were standing there saying them.

6. What does Baptism do for us?

Baptism forgives us our sins and ushers us into adoption into God's family. Jesus has attached His Word, His presence, to Baptism, so it is not something that the water, the pastor, or the person being baptized does or earns. It is Jesus' rich mercy attached to a physical Means of Grace that we get to experience. Just like Naaman's leprosy was washed away by bathing in the Jordan River, so also the disease of our sin is fully removed from us in our blessed washing.

7. What does the Lord's Supper do for us?

The Lord's Supper delivers Christ's very own body and blood to us in, with, and under the bread and the wine. It delivers forgiveness of sins, eternal life, unity with Christ, and unity with one another. It is not a good work or act meriting favor on the part of the recipient or the pastor, but is, like Baptism, a physical Means of Grace given to us by Christ to strengthen and comfort us.

8. Read 1 Corinthians 11:29–30. Why do pastors sometimes turn people away from the Lord's Supper?

Partaking of Communion in a wrong way, by failing to rightly recognize Jesus' presence or by living in open sin, is a sin. Misuse of the Lord's Supper had very bad effects on the people at Corinth, with some people even getting sick and dying! Pastors have been set as stewards, or guards, over the sacraments Jesus instituted, in order to make sure that they are properly observed. This is a huge responsibility, so give thanks for good pastors! If a pastor asks someone not to commune, he does so because he is trying to keep that person from sinning against Jesus' presence in the Sacrament.

9. How does Jesus' presence in the Sacraments affect our identity?

God understands our weakness and our desire for human contact, reassurance, and repetition. We do not need to reject these elements of our identity in order to appear strong or autonomous. Rather, God recognizes these needs and affirms them through the Sacraments, which minister to these needs and our identities as people who are both body and soul.

10. Where is Jesus now? Why is this important?

Jesus is present in His Word and Sacraments. This means that when we come to church, we are in the physical presence of God. God has not abandoned us, nor has He left us with a religion that is spiritualized or a God who is far from us. He comes down Sunday after Sunday into our midst to tend to our every need of soul and body.

CHAPTER FOUR

1. Jesus teaches us in Mark 13, among other things, to expect "wars and rumors of wars," natural disasters, famines, unrighteousness, false christs, and persecution. These have been true for Christians throughout church history, because the world is broken by sin and despises God's Word. How do you see examples of these in your own life? How do you see examples of these throughout history?

Answers will likely vary widely based on people's age and life experience. In general, though, all of us can identify examples of what Jesus is talking about in Mark 13. Violence, confusion, and death mar all life on earth until Christ's return, because all must bear the effects of sin.

2. How should we understand the Bible's prophecies about when Jesus will return?

The parts of the Bible that talk about the end times are often apocalyptic in genre, which means that they should not be read in a highly literal way (e.g., the one thousand years in Revelation means at a full and ready time, not an actual one thousand years). Similarly, discussions of Israel have to do with the people of God, not modern political boundaries, because Israel refers to the people of God, continuous across both Old and New Testaments. Likewise, it's important to remember that Jesus Himself tells us that the coming of the Last Day is a mystery to all and that only the Father knows when it will come.

3. **What two sets of categories can help us understand Scripture better?**

Any attempt to explain unclear passages of Scripture should be done using clear passages of Scripture. This is especially helpful when dealing with the end times since many of those texts are confusing. (See the discussion of understanding the "secret rapture" text in light of the flood in Genesis on pp. 144–46.) Additionally, we can use the categories of Law and Gospel—looking for God's Law and will for our life and God's promises of redemption through Christ—which were of immense value to the reformers. Using these categories can also help us navigate end-times prophecies, as we should treat them as Gospel for believers, a message of hope and salvation from our sin, rather than a list of things we need to do to bring about the end times ourselves.

4. **Read Matthew 25:31–46. Who are the sheep? Who are the goats? Why?**

The sheep are those who believe in Christ. They do good works because they are sheep (Christians), and that's just what sheep (Christians) do; they did not merit their "sheepiness" by doing good works. In contrast, the goats are those outside of Christ. They do not do good works in God's eyes because they are goats (non-Christians) and that's just what goats (non-Christians) do (or do not do); they cannot please God or merit salvation by anything they do, because they have rejected Christ's work to reconcile them with God.

5. **Read Matthew 13:47–50 and Matthew 25:41–46. What can we say about hell?**

Hell is the destination of those who reject Christ. It is a place of "weeping and gnashing of teeth," totally devoid of the presence of God. Since God is light and life and love, these things are absent from hell. Hell is not like the cartoonish depictions common in our culture; it is not a block party for rock stars nor a ghoulish torture chamber. It is more like solitary confinement. We are not told much more about hell, and it is unfruitful to speculate further.

6. Read Hebrews 4:9–10 and Revelation 14:13. What can we say about heaven?

Heaven is the dwelling of God, where the souls of the faithful rest with Him while awaiting the resurrection of all flesh. The faithful departed rest there, separated from their bodies but in absolute bliss and sinlessness. We do not know from Scripture whether or not the dead are aware of what goes on back on earth, though we do know from Scripture that the dead do not communicate with the living through visions, ghosts, and so on. Heaven as a resting place for the faithful, however, is temporary, as all people will be reunited with their bodies at the second coming of Christ.

7. Why are Christians neither Gnostics nor Epicureans?

Christians do not pit the human body and the human spirit against each other. Both are good in the eyes of God. Gnostics say that the material world is evil and the spirit is superior; Epicureans say that the material world is all that matters, and the spirit may not exist at all. Both go against the biblical doctrine that God proclaims the whole human person—body and soul—as "very good."

8. What happens "after heaven," when Jesus returns?

When Jesus returns, all flesh will be raised with incorruptible, deathless bodies to be judged. Those who rejected Christ will be sent to hell. Those who clung to Christ in faith will dwell with Him forever in the remade heavens and earth in perfection and righteousness.

9. What does Jesus' return tell us about our identity?

Our ultimate identity is the person we are in Christ—the man or woman who Christ will raise on the Last Day. Our maladies and sufferings do not define us, as they will be removed from us once and for all at the resurrection.

10. When is Jesus coming back? Why is this important?

We don't know when Jesus is coming back, but we know that He will return to raise and judge all flesh. This is good news for the Christian, because Jesus has not abandoned us to an infernal cycle of death and separation from our bodies, but instead, He will come to rectify all creation and restore to us the bliss known to our first parents before the fall.

CHAPTER FIVE

1. **How does God love us differently than we love things?**

   God doesn't just love humanity as an average or aggregate, like what we mean when we make general statements about "loving cats" or "loving Texas barbecue." Because we are limited, we can't actually have experienced everything within a category like this. God, however, is not limited, which means that when God says He loves the world (e.g., John 3:16), He means that He loves all of humanity as a whole as well as every single individual in a unique and omniscient way.

2. **What does it mean that Jesus died for the whole world?**

   Jesus didn't die just for the people who would end up saved or who "deserved it." Jesus died for the sins of everyone, even people who will reject Him. He could do this because He is God, and so He could atone for all of the sin of the world through His perfect innocence and righteousness.

3. **What does it mean that Jesus died for you?**

   Jesus died for you as an individual because He loves you as an individual. Jesus cares deeply for you as a unique person, a son or daughter of the Most High God, and for you, individually, did He die also. Because Jesus is also fully man, He can atone for your human soul.

4. **Read Luke 15, which contains the three parables of the lost sheep, the lost coin, and the lost son. What is the running theme between all three of these parables?**

   All three of these parables show us that Jesus cares about the children of God as individuals. No matter how far we stray, Jesus will come in search of us to bring us back to Him. Jesus' mercy endures all things because Jesus is perfect love and perfectly loves us all. (See also 1 Corinthians 13:4–8, which can be read in light of how Jesus depicts Himself in these parables.)

5. **Read Romans 8:38–39; Psalm 46:10; Matthew 28:20; and Hebrews 13:8. What do these verses tell us about Jesus and His love for us?**

   Jesus' love for us is never-ending, never-changing, never-ceasing. Nothing can remove us from His love or His presence.

6. How has God changed our hearts?

God has created in us new hearts—total new identities—hearts that can hear His Word and keep it, as well as share it with those around us. Our hearts previously were like stone—dead, deaf, unfeeling. But through the creative Word of Christ, our hearts have "grown ears," hearing His life-giving and life-creating Word.

7. How should we view the people around us?

Every person around us is a "you" for whom Christ has died. Every person around us not only bears the image of God given to all men but also has been redeemed at the high cost of Christ's very own holy blood.

8. What do we do now that Jesus has done it all?

We now share God's love with those around us by sharing the Good News of Jesus, as well as by serving in our daily roles, or vocations, through which God acts to love and provide for all people. We also continue to return to Christ in repentance when we fail to do these things and are continuously showered with His mercy and forgiveness.

9. What does Jesus' dying and rising for you tell us about our identities?

The world throws many distractions at us, and it can be difficult to see the universe-changing reality of Christ's work for us. We are worn out and confused by everything going on in our lives. But it is in the darkness that Jesus comes to us, shining His light to lighten our darkness and reminding us that He has already given us our new identity in Him as children of God who receive His good gifts.

10. Why did Jesus do all this? Why is this important?

Jesus did all of this—being born, living, dying, rising, ascending—for you. This totally unmerited sacrifice shows us God's great love—a love that we now have the privilege to share with others.